A Woman's Workshop on Proverbs

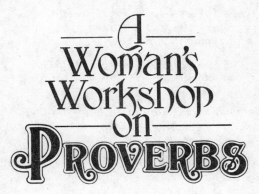

Books in this series—

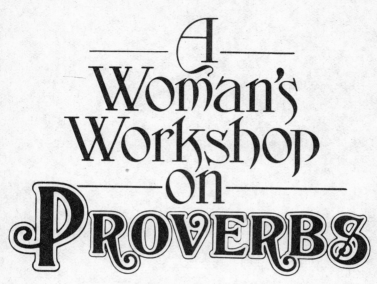

A Woman's Workshop on Proverbs

Student's Manual

Diane Bloem

ZONDERVAN
PUBLISHING HOUSE OF THE ZONDERVAN CORPORATION
GRAND RAPIDS, MICHIGAN 49506

The *King James Version* (KJV) is used as the basis for this Bible study. Other translations used are the *New International Version* (NIV), the *Revised Standard Version* (RSV), the *New English Bible* (NEB), and *The Living Bible* (LB).

A WOMAN'S WORKSHOP ON PROVERBS — STUDENT'S MANUAL

© 1978 by The Zondervan Corporation
Grand Rapids, Michigan

ISBN 0-310-21361-4

Printed in the United States of America

84   85   86   87   88 — 20   19   18   17   16   15   14

This book is lovingly dedicated
to my dear husband,

ROBERT C. BLOEM,

who experienced God's leading
through the Book of Proverbs
and shared this joy with me.
I thank the Lord for him.

CONTENTS

PREFACE

Proverbs on many subjects are scattered as sown seed throughout the Book of Proverbs. In this study manual they are carefully plucked and gathered into "theme-sheaves."

Of the many themes in Proverbs, I have chosen those which I felt were most profitable and adaptable for group discussion. I have composed discussion questions that will encourage individuals or groups to see these practical teachings in the context of the whole Bible and to explore various ways in which this distilled wisdom can be used in daily life.

I have studied this material with groups in eight churches, and I wish to thank all those group members for sharing their ideas and revelations with me so that this lesson material might be enriched.

I thank God for all He has taught me in the preparation of this book; and I pray that all who use this material may be richly blessed.

I also thank the Reverend Leonard Greenway, Th.M., Th.D., for his encouragement, for his suggestions, and for his evaluation and approval of this manuscript.

1

BACKGROUND

A proverb is a parable, a riddle, a taunt, or a perplexing statement. The distilling of a wise thought or statement into a few memorable words is a device used to arouse curiosity, sharpen wits, and provoke thought. All cultures in all ages have employed proverbs to express truth in a thought-provoking way. Ancient peoples had collections of proverbs similar to the Bible but without the strong religious emphasis; and Benjamin Franklin authored a book of proverbs in more modern times and called it *Poor Richard's Almanac*.

The Book of Proverbs is a book of practical ethics, which demonstrate that the Lord is interested in every aspect of life. It was written by Solomon, certain unnamed wise men, Agur the son of Jakeh, and King Lemuel and his mother. It is part of the body of biblical wisdom literature. It is also Hebrew poetry.

This type of poetry does not strive for rhythm or rhyme. Instead, it is poetry because it uses figurative speech and parallelism in thought. Parallelism is expressed in several ways: the repetition of similar ideas, the adding of a thought in the second line of a couplet, the presentation of a contrasting idea or thought in the second line, or the amplifying of the first line of thought in the second line of a couplet. Difficult passages in Proverbs can sometimes be clarified by analyzing the types of parallelism in the passage.

Proverbs are found throughout the Bible, especially in the teachings of Jesus. He quoted many Old Testament proverbs and used proverbs and parables as effective tools for teaching.

Our purpose in studying this book is to know the wisdom and the will of God for our lives. As we try to walk in God's way, may these studies guide and comfort us. "Every word of God proves true; he is a shield to those who take refuge in him" (Prov. 30:5 RSV).

DISCUSSION QUESTIONS

1. Can you find any proverbs in the Bible other than those found in the Book of Proverbs? Read, for example, 1 Samuel 24:13; Psalm 69:10-11; Luke 4:23. _____

   _____

   _____

   _____

2. Can you find any verses in the Sermon on the Mount (Matt. 5–7) which have become modern proverbs? _____

   _____

   _____

   _____

   _____

3. The parable in Luke 10:25-37 has a well-known title. The title itself has become a proverb carrying the essence of the parable in three words. What is the name of that parable and what does the name imply? _____

   _____

   _____

4. Why is it important that Jesus and the apostles quoted from the Book of Proverbs? Compare Matthew 15:4 with Proverbs 20:20; Romans 12:20 with Proverbs 25:21-22; James 4:6 with Proverbs 3:34; and 1 Peter 4:8 with Proverbs 10:12. _____

_____

_____

_____

_____

5. Scan the Book of Proverbs and try to determine its "tone." Is it one of anger, rebuke, concern, patience, love, gaiety, or frustration? _____

_____

6. How can the Book of Proverbs best be studied—in public or in private? Should it be read a chapter at a time? Why or why not? _____

_____

_____

_____

7. What do you expect to learn about God in the study of this book? _____

_____

_____

_____

2

JOY

"Happy is the man that findeth wisdom, and the man that getteth understanding. . . . Her ways are ways of pleasantness, and all her paths are peace. She is a tree of life to them that lay hold upon her: and happy is every one that retaineth her" (Proverbs 3:13,17-18).

"Let thy fountain be blessed: and rejoice with the wife of thy youth" (5:18).

"Then I [Wisdom] was by him, as one brought up with him: and I was daily his delight, rejoicing always before him; Rejoicing in the habitable part of his earth; and my delights were with the sons of men. Now therefore hearken unto me, O ye children: for blessed are they that keep my ways. Hear instruction, and be wise, and refuse it not. Blessed is the man that heareth me, watching daily at my gates, waiting at the posts of my doors" (8:30-34).

"The hope of the righteous shall be gladness: but the expectation of the wicked shall perish" (10:28).

"When it goeth well with the righteous, the city rejoiceth: and when the wicked perish, there is shouting. . . . They that are of a froward heart are abomination to the LORD: but such as are upright in their way are his delight" (11:10,20).

"Deceit is in the heart of them that imagine evil: but to the counsellors of peace is joy. . . . Heaviness in the heart of man maketh it stoop: but a good word maketh it glad" (12:20,25).

"The light of the righteous rejoiceth: but the lamp of the wicked shall be put out. . . . Hope deferred maketh the heart sick: but when the desire cometh, it is a tree of life. . . . The desire accomplished is sweet to the soul: but it is abomination to fools to depart from evil" (13:9,12,19).

"The heart knoweth his own bitterness: and a stranger doth not intermeddle with his joy. . . . Even in laughter the heart is sorrowful; and the end of that mirth is heaviness. . . . He that despiseth his neighbor sinneth: but he that hath mercy on the poor, happy is he" (14:10,13,21).

"A merry heart maketh a cheerful countenance: but by sorrow of the heart the spirit is broken. . . . All the days of the afflicted are evil: but he that is of a merry heart hath a continual feast. . . . Folly is joy to him that is destitute of wisdom: but a man of understanding walketh uprightly. . . . A man hath joy by the answer of his mouth: and a word spoken in due season, how good is it! . . . The light of the eyes rejoiceth the heart: and a good report maketh the bones fat" (15:13,15,21,23,30).

"He that handleth a matter wisely shall find good: and whoso trusteth in the Lord, happy is he. . . . Pleasant words are as a honeycomb, sweet to the soul, and health to the bones" (16:20,24).

"He that begetteth a fool doeth it to his sorrow: and the father of a fool hath no joy. A merry heart doeth good like a medicine: but a broken spirit drieth the bones" (17:21,22).

"My son, if thine heart be wise, my heart shall rejoice, even mine. Yea, my reins shall rejoice, when thy lips speak right things. . . . The father of the righteous shall greatly rejoice: and he that begetteth a wise child shall have joy of him. Thy father and thy mother shall be glad, and she that bare thee shall rejoice" (23:15-16,24-25).

"Rejoice not when thine enemy falleth, and let not thine heart be glad when he stumbleth: Lest the Lord see it, and it displease him, and he turn away his wrath from him" (24:17-18).

"As cold waters to a thirsty soul, so is good news from a far country" (25:25).

"Ointment and perfume rejoice the heart: so doth the sweetness of a man's friend by hearty counsel. . . . My son, be wise, and make my heart glad, that I may answer him that reproacheth me" (27:9,11).

"When righteous men do rejoice, there is great glory: but when the wicked rise, a man is hidden. . . . Happy is the man that feareth alway: but he that hardeneth his heart shall fall into mischief" (28:12,14).

"When the righteous are in authority, the people rejoice: but when the wicked beareth rule, the people mourn. Whoso loveth wisdom rejoiceth his father: but he that keepeth company with harlots spendeth his substance. . . . In the transgression of an evil man there is a snare: but the righteous doth sing and rejoice. . . . Correct thy son, and he shall give thee rest: yea, he shall give delight unto thy soul. Where there is no vision, the people perish: but he that keepeth the law, happy is he" (29:2,3,6,17,18).

[The virtuous woman:] "Strength and honor are her clothing; and she shall rejoice in time to come" (31:25).

CASTING LIGHT ON THESE VERSES

1. Underline all the words in these verses that refer to joy.
2. In these verses, what things are mentioned that bring joy?

_____

_____

_____

_____

3. What things are mentioned that give God joy?_____

_____

4. Two verses tell of things that do not or should not give us joy. What are they? _____

_____

_____

5. Read the following verses in several versions of the Bible: 5:18; 8:30-34; 13:9; 14:13; 15:15,30; 29:18; 31:25.

MORE LIGHT FROM THE BIBLE

6. What is meant by the word *merry?* (15:13,15; 17:22). Compare the verses in Proverbs with the following: Genesis 43:34; Ruth 3:7; 1 Kings 21:7; 2 Chronicles 7:10; Ecclesiastes 10:19; Jeremiah 30:19; Luke 15:32; James 5:13. _____

_____

_____

_____

_____

_____

7. Find ten verses in other parts of the Bible that mention joy. (Your Bible concordance will help you.) Reflect on the

elements of joy as you find them in these verses. _____

_____

_____

_____

_____

_____

8. There are many kinds of laughter mentioned in the Bible. Find some of these in the following verses: Genesis 17:17; 18:12-15; Nehemiah 2:19; Job 5:22; Luke 6:21,25; James 4:9. _____

_____

_____

_____

   a. When the Bible speaks of God's laughter, does it express joy or judgment? See Psalms 2:4; 37:13; 59:8.
   _____

   b. Why is Proverbs 1:26 not included in our lesson theme? _____

   _____

9. Was Jesus happy? See John 15:11 and Hebrews 12:2.
   _____

10. Read James 1:2; Hebrews 12:11; 1 Peter 4:13. Should we desire suffering? _____

   _____

11. Is Christian joy quiet or noisy or both? Consider Psalms 5:11; 63:5-7; 95:1-3; James 1:2; 5:13. _____

_____

12. Proverbs 13:9 and 15:30 refer to light. Explore the meaning of these verses by comparing them with Psalms 27:1; 38:10; 97:11; 119:105; Proverbs 4:18; 6:23; Micah 7:8; Matthew 6:23. _____

_____

_____

_____

_____

LIGHT FOR OUR LIVES

13. Since life is serious business, should Christians laugh and have fun?_____

_____

14. Should our worship services be happy or serious and solemn? _____

_____

15. Do most of the Christians you know seem to be happy? Are you a happy Christian? _____

_____

_____

16. How is joy important in our witness for the Lord? Give examples. _____

_____

_____

_____

_____

17. Does joy weaken us in our fight against sin? _____

_____

_____

18. Should Christians tell jokes? If so, what kind?_____

_____

19. Does the Bible approve of parties, etc.? Prove your answer. _____

_____

_____

_____

3

WEALTH AND POVERTY

"Honor the Lord with thy substance, and with the firstfruits of all thine increase: So shall thy barns be filled with plenty, and thy presses shall burst out with new wine. . . . Happy is the man that findeth wisdom, and the man that getteth understanding. . . . Length of days is in her right hand; and in her left hand riches and honor" (Proverbs 3:9-10,13,16).

"Riches and honor are with me [Wisdom]; yea, durable riches and righteousness" (8:18).

"He becometh poor that dealeth with a slack hand: but the hand of the diligent maketh rich. . . . The rich man's wealth is his strong city: the destruction of the poor is their poverty. . . . The blessing of the Lord, it maketh rich, and he addeth no sorrow with it" (10:4,15,22).

"Riches profit not in the day of wrath: but righteousness delivereth from death. . . . There is that scattereth, and yet increaseth; and there is that withholdeth more than is meet, but it tendeth to poverty. The liberal soul shall be made fat: and he that watereth shall be watered also himself. He that withholdeth corn, the people shall curse him: but blessing shall be upon the head of him that selleth it. . . . He that trusteth in his riches shall fall: but the righteous shall flourish as a branch" (11:4,24-26,28).

"There is that maketh himself rich, yet hath nothing: there is that maketh himself poor, yet hath great riches. The ransom of a man's life are his riches: but the poor heareth not rebuke. . . . Wealth gotten by vanity shall be diminished: but he that gathereth by labor shall increase. . . . Poverty and shame shall be to him that refuseth instruction: but he that regardeth reproof shall be honored. . . . A good man leaveth an inheritance to his children's children: and the wealth of the sinner is laid up for the just. Much food is in the tillage of the poor: but there is that is destroyed for want of judgment" (13:7-8,11,18,22,23).

"The poor is hated even of his own neighbor: but the rich hath many friends. He that despiseth his neighbor sinneth: but he that hath mercy on the poor, happy is he. . . . The crown of the wise is their riches: but the foolish ness of fools is folly. . . . He that oppresseth the poor reproacheth his Maker: but he that honoreth him hath mercy on the poor" (14:20,21,24,31).

"Better is a little with righteousness than great revenues without right" (16:8).

"Whoso mocketh the poor reproacheth his Maker: and he that is glad at calamities shall not be unpunished" (17:5).

"The rich man's wealth is his strong city, and as a high wall in his own conceit. . . . The poor useth entreaties; but the rich answereth roughly" (18:11,23).

"Better is the poor that walketh in his integrity, than he that is perverse in his lips, and is a fool. . . . Wealth maketh many friends; but the poor is separated from his neighbor. . . . All the brethren of the poor do hate him: how much more do his friends go far from him? he pursueth them with words, yet they are wanting to him. . . . House and riches are the inheritance of fathers: and a prudent wife is from the Lord. . . . He that hath pity upon the poor lendeth unto the Lord; and that which he hath given will he pay him again. . . . The desire of a man is his kindness: and a poor man is better than a liar" (19:1,4,7,14,17,22).

"Whoso stoppeth his ears at the cry of the poor, he also shall cry himself, but shall not be heard. . . . He that loveth pleasure shall be a poor man: he that loveth wine and oil shall not be rich" (21:13,17).

"A good name is rather to be chosen than great riches, and loving favor rather than silver and gold. The rich and poor meet together: the Lord is the maker of them all. . . . By humility and the fear of the Lord are riches, and honor, and life. . . . The rich ruleth over the poor, and the borrower is servant to the lender. . . . He that hath a bountiful eye shall be blessed; for he giveth of his bread to the poor. . . . He that oppresseth the poor to increase his riches, and he that giveth to the rich, shall surely come to want. . . . Rob not the poor, because he is poor; neither oppress the afflicted in the gate: For the Lord will plead their cause, and spoil the soul of those that spoiled them" (22:1,2,4,7,9,16,22-23).

"Labor not to be rich: cease from thine own wisdom. Wilt thou set thine eyes upon that which is not? for riches certainly make themselves wings; they fly away as an eagle toward heaven. . . . For the drunkard and the glutton shall come to poverty: and drowsiness shall clothe a man with rags" (23:4,5,21).

"By knowledge shall the chambers be filled with all precious and pleasant riches" (24:4).

"Be thou diligent to know the state of thy flocks, and look well to thy herds. For riches are not for ever: and doth the crown endure to every generation?" (27:23-24).

"A poor man that oppresseth the poor is like a sweeping rain which leaveth no food. . . . Better is the poor that walketh in his uprightness, than he that is perverse in his ways, though he be rich. . . . He that by usury and unjust gain increaseth his substance, he shall gather it for him that will pity the poor. . . . As a roaring lion, and a ranging bear; so is a wicked ruler over the poor people. . . . He that tilleth his land shall have plenty of bread: but he that followeth after vain persons shall have poverty enough. A faithful man shall abound with blessings: but he that maketh haste to be rich shall not be innocent. . . . He that hasteth to be rich hath an evil eye, and considereth not that poverty shall come upon him. . . . He that giveth unto the poor shall not lack: but he that hideth his eyes shall have many a curse" (28:3,6,8, 15,19,20,22,27).

"Remove far from me vanity and lies: give me neither poverty nor riches; feed me with food convenient for me: Lest I be full, and deny thee, and say, Who is the LORD? or lest I be poor, and steal, and take the name of my God in vain. . . . There is a generation, whose teeth are as swords, and their jaw teeth as knives, to devour the poor from off the earth, and the needy from among men" (30:8-9,14).

"[The virtuous woman] stretcheth out her hand to the poor; yea, she reacheth forth her hands to the needy" (31:20).

CASTING LIGHT ON THESE VERSES

1. According to 3:9-10 and 10:22, the Lord rewards the righteous with riches. What other factors are suggested in our lesson which tend to make one wealthy? _____

_____

_____

_____

_____

2. List at least five things that you can learn from these verses about poor people or the state of poverty. _____

_____

_____

_____

_____

_____

3. Find at least three verses which teach us to have concern for the poor. _____

   _____

   _____

   _____

4. List at least five verses which point out the foolishness of striving for riches. _____

   _____

   _____

   _____

   _____

   _____

5. According to these verses, how can one be happy and rich? _____

   _____

   _____

6. Do these verses teach that wealth is the ideal economic state for life? Prove your answer. _____

   _____

   _____

   _____

MORE LIGHT FROM THE BIBLE

7. Name at least three devout believers from the Old Testament period whom the Lord blessed with riches. _____

_____

_____

8. What provision did God make for the care of the poor? See Exodus 23:11; Leviticus 19:10; 23:22 (cf. Ruth 2:2); Psalm 41:1-3; Proverbs 28:27; Matthew 19:21; Luke 14:12-14. _____

_____

_____

9. What special comfort for poor people is found in Psalms 12:5 and 140:12? _____

_____

10. What reasons can you give for the truth expressed in Deuteronomy 15:11 and Matthew 26:11?_____

_____

_____

11. What sin is vividly denounced by the prophets in Isaiah 3:14-15; Ezekiel 16:49; and Amos 2:6; 5:11-12? _____

_____

_____

12. What are we instructed to remember according to Deuteronomy 8:11-20 and 1 Samuel 2:7-8?_____

_____

_____

13. What does Jesus teach in Matthew 13:22? _____

in Mark 12:41-44? _____

_____

in Luke 18:24-27? _____

_____

14. What is meant by Paul's statement in 1 Corinthians 10:24?

_____

_____

15. Why is there discrimination against poor people in the church? See James 2:1-9 and Proverbs 22:16. _____

_____

_____

16. What truth is "driven home" in Jeremiah 9:23-24? _____

_____

_____

LIGHT FOR OUR LIVES

17. If you are not rich, are you blessed? _____

_____

18. What special blessings are enjoyed by the poor? _____

_____

_____

19. What economic condition would you choose as ideal?

_____

_____

20. Today, too, the church hears the cry of the poor. What is being done in response to this cry? What are you doing as part of this response? What more should and can be done?

_____

_____

_____

_____

_____

4

OLD AGE/LONG LIFE

"My son, forget not my law; but let thine heart keep my commandments: For length of days, and long life, and peace, shall they add to thee. . . . Happy is the man that findeth wisdom, and the man that getteth understanding. . . . Length of days is in her right hand; and in her left hand riches and honor" (Proverbs 3:1-2,13,16).

"Hear, O my son, and receive my sayings: and the years of thy life shall be many" (4:10).

"For by me thy days shall be multiplied, and the years of thy life shall be increased" (9:11).

"The labor of the righteous tendeth to life: the fruit of the wicked to sin. He is in the way of life that keepeth instruction: but he that refuseth reproof erreth. . . . The fear of the LORD prolongeth days: but the years of the wicked shall be shortened. . . . The righteous shall never be removed: but the wicked shall not inhabit the earth" (10:16,17,27,30).

"Riches profit not in the day of wrath: but righteousness delivereth from death. . . . As righteousness tendeth to life: so he that pursueth evil pursueth it to his own death" (11:4,19).

"In the way of righteousness is life; and in the pathway thereof there is no death" (12:28).

"He that keepeth his mouth keepeth his life: but he that openeth wide his lips shall have destruction" (13:3).

"A sound heart is the life of the flesh: but envy the rottenness of the bones" (14:30).

"Understanding is a wellspring of life unto him that hath it: but the instruction of fools is folly. . . . The hoary head is a crown of glory, if it be found in the way of righteousness" (16:22,31).

"Children's children are the crown of old men; and the glory of children are their fathers" (17:6).

"The fear of the LORD tendeth to life: and he that hath it shall abide satisfied; he shall not be visited with evil" (19:23).

"The glory of young men is their strength: and the beauty of old men is the gray head" (20:29).

"By humility and the fear of the LORD are riches, and honor, and life. . . . Train up a child in the way he should go: and when he is old, he will not depart from it" (22:4,6).

"Hearken unto thy father that begat thee, and despise not thy mother when she is old" (23:22).

"The prince that wanteth understanding is also a great oppressor: but he that hateth covetousness shall prolong his days" (28:16).

"[The virtuous woman]: Strength and honor are her clothing; and she shall rejoice in time to come" (31:25).

CASTING LIGHT ON THESE VERSES

1. What things that ensure long life are mentioned in these verses? _____

    _____

    _____

    _____

2. Who is speaking in 9:11? (See the context.) _____

    _____

3. Righteousness is mentioned in several places (e.g., 11:19; 12:28) as ensuring long life. What is meant by righteousness? Is long life a reward for right living? See also Job 12:20; 21:7. _____

    _____

    _____

    _____

4. What is a "sound heart" (14:30)? _____

    _____

5. What is a "hoary head" (16:31)? Is this verse true today? See also 20:29. Is there less or more respect for older people today than in years past? _____

   _____

   _____

   _____

   _____

6. Express 17:6 in your own words. _____

   _____

   What are we told about the joys of having grandchildren? See Ruth 4:14-16. _____

   _____

7. Express 22:6 in your own words. What does this verse tell us about old age? _____

   _____

   _____

8. Read 23:22. How long does one have to listen to or obey his parents? _____

   _____

   Is the placing of elderly parents in institutions indicative of despising them? Why or why not? _____

   _____

   _____

   How does God judge this matter? _____

   _____

9. How would coveting affect the length of one's life (28:16)?

_____

10. Read chapter 31. Then read verse 25 in other versions. What does this verse tell us about old age?_____

_____

_____

MORE LIGHT FROM THE BIBLE

11. Read the Ten Commandments (Exod. 20:1-17). What is the "first commandment with promise" (Eph. 6:2)? What is that promise? _____

_____

_____

12. What can you tell us about the old age of these Bible characters?
    a. Isaac (Gen. 27; 31:41; 35:28-29)._____

    _____

    _____

    b. Jacob (Gen. 45:25-28; 46:1-5; 47:7-12,28-31; 49:33)._____

    _____

    _____

    c. Joshua (Josh. 13:1; 23:1-9; 24:22-30). _____

    _____

    _____

d. David (1 Kings 1:1-4,15ff.,28-31; 2:1-4,10-11; Ps. 37:23-28). _____

_____

_____

_____

e. Solomon (1 Kings 11:4-6). _____

_____

f. Anna (Luke 2:36-39). _____

_____

13. What adjective in the KJV and RSV describes the old age of each of these men: Abraham (Gen. 25:8), Gideon (Judg. 8:32), and David (1 Chron. 29:28)? Why?_____

_____

_____

14. What do we learn about old age in the following verses?

a. Psalm 148:12-13. _____

b. Jeremiah 31:13. _____

c. Joel 2:28._____

d. Psalm 92:14._____

15. What advice does 1 Peter 5:5 give to help young and old get along well with each other?_____

_____

16. What special tasks does the Lord have for old people? See

Psalm 78:3-7; Joel 1:2-3; 1 Timothy 5:9-10; Titus 2:1-5.

_____

_____

_____

_____

17. Ecclesiastes 12:1-7 is a poetic picture of old age. How many parts of the body can you identify in it? _____

_____

_____

_____

18. Read Psalm 71, the aged man's prayer and praise. _____

_____

LIGHT FOR OUR LIVES

19. Do most people today regard long life as a blessing? ___

_____

20. How does one's life-walk (godly or ungodly) affect one's old age?_____

_____

_____

21. Are very old ungodly people being especially blessed by God? _____

_____

22. Should we, or may we, ask God for long life? Why or why not? _____

_____

_____

_____

23. Is the emphasis on youth as we see it today good for our social structure? _____

_____

_____

24. Is it good to have young elders in the church? Is it necessary?_____

_____

_____

25. How can elderly Christians be useful and happy? Give some specific, practical suggestions._____

_____

_____

_____

26. Does the segregation of elderly people into retirement homes, villages, colonies (Florida), etc., enhance their usefulness in God's kingdom? _____

_____

_____

27. Why do people often treat their elderly parents as children? Is this honoring them? _____

_____

_____

28. How can we prepare for a good old age? _____

_____

_____

_____

29. How can we brighten old age for others? _____

_____

_____

_____

30. What kind of old person do you want to be? _____

_____

_____

5

JUSTICE AND GOVERNMENT

"By me kings reign, and princes decree justice. By me princes rule, and nobles, even all the judges of the earth. . . . I lead in the way of righteousness, in the midst of the paths of judgment" (Proverbs 8:15-16,20).

"A false balance is abomination to the LORD: but a just weight is his delight. . . . A hypocrite with his mouth destroyeth his neighbor: but through knowledge shall the just be delivered. When it goeth well with the righteous, the city rejoiceth: and when the wicked perish there is shouting. By the blessing of the upright the city is exalted: but it is overthrown by the mouth of the wicked. . . . Where no counsel is, the people fall: but in the multitude of counsellors there is safety" (11:1,9-11,14).

"There shall no evil happen to the just: but the wicked shall be filled with mischief. . . . The hand of the diligent shall bear rule: but the slothful shall be under tribute" (12:21,24).

"A faithful witness will not lie: but a false witness will utter lies. . . . A true witness delivereth souls: but a deceitful witness speaketh lies. . . . In the multitude of people is the king's honor: but in the want of people is the destruction of the prince. . . . He that oppresseth the poor reproacheth his Maker: but he that honoreth him hath mercy on the poor. . . . Righteousness exalteth a nation: but sin is a reproach to any people. The king's favor is toward a wise servant; but his wrath is against him that causeth shame" (14:5,25,28,31,34,35).

"Without counsel purposes are disappointed: but in the multitude of counsellors they are established. . . . He that is greedy of gain troubleth his own house; but he that hateth gifts shall live" (15:22,27).

"When a man's ways please the LORD, he maketh even his enemies to be at peace with him. Better is a little with righteousness than great revenues without right. . . . A divine sentence is in the lips of the king: his mouth transgresseth not in judgment. A just weight and balance are the Lord's: all the weights of the bag are his work. It is an abomination to kings to commit wickedness: for the throne is established by righteousness. Righteous lips are the delight of kings; and they love him that speaketh right. The wrath of a king is as messengers of death: but a wise man will pacify it. In the light of the king's countenance is life; and his favor is as a cloud of the latter rain. . . . He that is slow to anger is better than the mighty; and he that ruleth his spirit than he that taketh a city. The lot is cast into the lap; but the whole disposing thereof is of the Lord" (16:7-8,10-15,32,33).

"Excellent speech becometh not a fool: much less do lying lips a prince. A gift is as a precious stone in the eyes of him that hath it: whithersoever it turneth, it prospereth. . . . He that justifieth the wicked, and he that condemneth the just, even they both are abomination to the Lord. . . . A wicked man taketh a gift out of the bosom to pervert the ways of judgment. . . . Also to punish the just is not good, nor to strike princes for equity" (17:7,8, 15,23,26).

"A false witness shall not be unpunished, and he that speaketh lies shall not escape. Many will entreat the favor of the prince: and every man is a friend to him that giveth gifts. . . . A false witness shall not be unpunished, and he that speaketh lies shall perish. Delight is not seemly for a fool; much less for a servant to have rule over princes. . . . The king's wrath is as the roaring of a lion; but his favor is as dew upon the grass. . . . An ungodly witness scorneth judgment: and the mouth of the wicked devoureth iniquity. Judgments are prepared for scorners, and stripes for the back of fools" (19:5,6,9,10,12,28,29).

The fear of a king is as the roaring of a lion: whoso provoketh him to anger sinneth against his own soul. . . . A king that sitteth in the throne of judgment scattereth away all evil with his eyes. . . . Divers weights, and divers measures, both of them are alike abomination to the Lord. . . . Every purpose is established by counsel: and with good advice make war. . . . Divers weights are an abomination unto the Lord; and a false balance is not good. . . . A wise king scattereth the wicked, and bringeth the wheel over them. . . . Mercy and truth preserve the king: and his throne is upholden by mercy" (20:2,8,10,18,23,26,28).

"The king's heart is in the hand of the Lord, as the rivers of water:he turneth it whithersoever he will. . . . To do justice and judgment is more acceptable to the Lord than sacrifice" (21:1,3).

"He that loveth pureness of heart, for the grace of his lips the king shall be his friend. . . . Remove not the ancient landmark, which thy fathers have set. Seest thou a man diligent in his business? he shall stand before kings; he shall not stand before mean men" (22:11,28,29).

"A wise man is strong; yea, a man of knowledge increaseth strength. For by wise counsel thou shalt make thy war: and in multitude of counsellors there is safety. . . . My son, fear thou the Lord and the king: and meddle not with them that are given to change: For their calamity shall rise suddenly; and who knoweth the ruin of them both? These things also belong to the wise. It is not good to have respect of persons in judgment. He that saith unto the wicked, Thou art righteous; him shall the people curse, nations shall abhor him: But to them that rebuke him shall be delight, and a good blessing shall come upon them" (24:5,6,21-25).

"It is the glory of God to conceal a thing: but the honor of kings is to search out a matter. The heaven for height, and the earth for depth, and the heart of kings is unsearchable. Take away the dross from the silver, and there shall come forth a vessel for the finer. Take away the wicked from before the king, and his throne shall be established in righteousness. Put not forth thyself in the presence of the king, and stand not in the place of great men: For better it is that it be said unto thee, Come up hither; than that thou shouldest be put lower in the presence of the prince whom thine eyes have seen. . . . By long forbearing is a prince persuaded, and a soft tongue breaketh the bone" (25:2-7,15).

"For the transgression of a land many are the princes thereof: but by a man of understanding and knowledge the state thereof shall be prolonged. . . . They that forsake the law praise the wicked: but such as keep the law contend with them. Evil men understand not judgment: but they that seek the LORD understand all things. . . . Whoso keepeth the law is a wise son: but he that is a companion of riotous men shameth his father. He that by usury and unjust gain increaseth his substance, he shall gather it for him that will pity the poor. . . . When righteous men do rejoice, there is great glory: but when the wicked rise, a man is hidden. . . . As a roaring lion, and a ranging bear; so is a wicked ruler over the poor people. The prince that wanteth understanding is also a great oppressor: but he that hateth covetousness shall prolong his days. . . . To have respect of persons is not good: for for a piece of bread that man will transgress" (28:2,4,5,7,8,12,15,16,21).

"When the righteous are in authority, the people rejoice: but when the wicked beareth rule, the people mourn. . . . The king by judgment establisheth the land: but he that receiveth gifts overthroweth it. . . . Scornful men bring a city into a snare: but wise men turn away wrath. . . . The bloodthirsty hate the upright: but the just seek his soul. . . . If a ruler hearken to lies, all his servants are wicked. . . . The king that faithfully judgeth the poor, his throne shall be established forever. . . . When the wicked are multiplied, transgression increaseth: but the righteous shall see their fall. . . . Many seek the ruler's favor; but every man's judgment cometh from the LORD. An unjust man is an abomination to the wicked" (29:2,4,8,10,12,14,16,26,27).

"Give not thy strength unto women, nor thy ways to that which destroyeth kings. It is not for kings, O Lemuel, it is not for kings to drink wine; nor for princes strong drink: Lest they drink, and forget the law, and pervert the judgment of any of the afflicted. . . . Open thy mouth for the dumb in the cause of all such as are appointed to destruction. Open thy mouth, judge righteously, and plead the cause of the poor and needy" (31:3-5,8-9).

CASTING LIGHT ON THESE VERSES

1. When these verses speak of a "just man" (11:9; 12:21; 17:26; 21:15; 29:27), does this necessarily mean a righteous man—a Christian? Explain. _____

   _____

   _____

2. Are Christians ever false witnesses (14:5,25; 19:5,9,28)? Can any but Christians ever be truly bound by the oath that is administered in our courts? Why or why not?_____

   _____

   _____

3. If no evil will befall the just (12:21), how can you explain the fact that there have been so many Christian martyrs?

   _____

   _____

4. Explain 14:28. _____

   _____

5. See 14:31 and 24:23-24. Do you believe that poor people and minority groups receive justice in our courts?_____

   _____

6. What is meant by "gift" in 15:27; 17:8,23: 19:6; 29:4?

   _____

   _____

   What are the dangers posed in the receiving of favors, such as use of an airplane, etc.? _____

_____

_____

7. According to these verses, what qualities should rulers
   have? _____

   _____

   _____

   _____

   _____

8. Which verses point out the need for wise and righteous
   advisors in government? _____

   _____

   _____

   Can you cite any instances in history in which rulers were

   influenced by bad advice? _____

   _____

   _____

9. May our country expect peace if we elect Christians to
   public office (16:7-8; 29:2,10)? _____

   _____

10. May Christians participate or engage in civil disobedience
    (24:21-22)? _____

    _____

11. Which verses assure us that God is in control? _____

    _____

MORE LIGHT FROM THE BIBLE

12. Read Romans 13:1-7; Titus 3:1; 1 Peter 2:13-17. Should Christians revolt against wicked governments? _____

    _____

    _____

13. Jesus said, "Judge not that ye be not judged" (See Matt. 7:1-5). Does this passage teach that Christians should not serve on juries?_____

    _____

    _____

14. Justice and righteousness go hand in hand (Isa. 1:21; 5:7; 9:7; 16:5; 32:1,16; 33:5). How can Christians work for justice in schools, in business dealings, in international affairs? _____

    _____

    _____

    _____

15. What does the term *justification* mean? See Romans 5:15-19. _____

    _____

16. Show how God's plan of justification was accomplished within the framework of the law. See Hebrews 9:22. __

    _____

17. Why can you be glad that Jesus is coming to judge the living and the dead (Acts 10:42)? See also Acts 17:31; 1

Thessalonians 4:16-18; 2 Thessalonians 1:3-10; 1 Peter
4:1-7. _____

_____

_____

LIGHT FOR OUR LIVES

18. If you see a crime committed or an accident occur, should
    you volunteer to be a witness? _____

    _____

    _____

19. Why are law enforcement agencies not highly respected
    today? _____

    _____

    _____

20. How can we teach respect for law? _____

    _____

    _____

6

REPROOF AND ADVICE

"Turn you at my reproof: behold, I will pour out my spirit unto you, I will make known my words unto you. Because I have called, and ye refused; I have stretched out my hand, and no man regarded; But ye have set at naught all my counsel, and would none of my reproof: I also will laugh at your calamity; I will mock when your fear cometh; When your fear cometh as desolation, and your destruction cometh as a whirlwind; when distress and anguish cometh upon you. Then shall they call upon me, but I will not answer; they shall seek me early, but they shall not find me: For that they hated knowledge, and did not choose the fear of the LORD: They would none of my counsel: they despised all my reproof. Therefore shall they eat of the fruit of their own way, and be filled with their own devices" (Proverbs 1:23-31).

"My son, despise not the chastening of the LORD; neither be weary of his correction: For whom the LORD loveth he correcteth; even as a father the son in whom he delighteth" (3:11-12).

"Hear me now therefore, O ye children, . . . Lest thou give thine honor unto others, and thy years unto the cruel: . . . And thou mourn at the last, . . . And say, How have I hated instruction, and my heart despised reproof; And have not obeyed the voice of my teachers, nor inclined mine ear to them that instructed me! I was almost in all evil in the midst of the congregation and assembly. . . . His own iniquities shall take the wicked himself, and he shall be holden with the cords of his sins. He shall die without instruction; and in the greatness of his folly he shall go astray" (5:7a,9,11a,12-14,22-23).

"For the commandment is a lamp; and the law is light; and reproofs of instruction are the way of life. . . ." (6:23).

"He that reproveth a scorner getteth to himself shame: and he that rebuketh a wicked man getteth himself a blot. Reprove not a scorner, lest he hate thee: rebuke a wise man, and he will love thee" (9:7,8).

"He is in the way of life that keepeth instruction: but he that refuseth reproof erreth" (10:17).

"Whoso loveth instruction loveth knowledge: but he that hateth reproof is brutish. . . . The way of a fool is right in his own eyes: but he that hearkeneth unto counsel is wise" (12:1,15).

"A wise son heareth his father's instruction: but a scorner heareth not rebuke. . . . Only by pride cometh contention: but with the well advised is wisdom. . . . Poverty and shame shall be to him that refuseth instruction: but he that regardeth reproof shall be honored" (13:1,10,18).

"A wise man feareth, and departeth from evil: but the fool rageth and is confident" (14:16, cf. RSV).

"A fool despiseth his father's instruction: but he that regardeth reproof is prudent. . . . Correction is grievous unto him that forsaketh the way: and he that hateth reproof shall die. . . . A scorner loveth not one that reproveth him: neither will he go unto the wise. . . . The ear that heareth the reproof of life abideth among the wise. He that refuseth instruction despiseth his own soul: but he that heareth reproof getteth understanding" (15:5,10,12,31,32).

"A reproof entereth more into a wise man than a hundred stripes into a fool" (17:10).

"Hear counsel, and receive instruction, that thou mayest be wise in thy latter end. . . . Smite a scorner, and the simple will beware: and reprove one that hath understanding, and he will understand knowledge" (19:20,25).

"The blueness of a wound cleanseth away evil: so do stripes the inward parts of the belly" (20:30).

"When the scorner is punished, the simple is made wise: and when the wise is instructed, he receiveth knowledge" (21:11).

"Have not I written to thee excellent things in counsels and knowledge, That I might make thee know the certainty of the words of truth; that thou mightest answer the words of truth to them that send unto thee?" (22:20-21).

"Withhold not correction from the child: for if thou beatest him with the rod, he shall not die. Thou shalt beat him with the rod, and shalt deliver his soul from hell" (23:13-14).

"He that saith unto the wicked, Thou art righteous; him shall the people curse, nations shall abhor him: But to them that rebuke him shall be delight, and a good blessing shall come upon them" (24:24-25).

"As an earring of gold, and an ornament of fine gold, so is a wise reprover upon an obedient ear" (25:12).

"A whip for the horse, a bridle for the ass, and a rod for the fool's back" (26:3).

"Open rebuke is better than secret love. Faithful are the wounds of a friend; but the kisses of an enemy are deceitful. . . . My son, be wise, and make my heart glad, that I may answer him that reproacheth me" (27:5,6,11).

"He that rebuketh a man afterwards shall find more favor than he that flattereth with the tongue" (28:23).

"He, that being often reproved hardeneth his neck, shall suddenly be destroyed, and that without remedy. . . . The rod and reproof give wisdom: but a child left to himself bringeth his mother to shame. . . . Correct thy son, and he shall give thee rest; yea, he shall give delight unto thy soul. . . . A servant will not be corrected by words: for though he understand he will not answer" (29:1,15,17,19).

"Every word of God is pure: he is a shield unto them that put their trust in him. Add thou not unto his words, lest he reprove thee, and thou be found a liar" (30:5-6).

CASTING LIGHT ON THESE VERSES

1. What is reproof? What are some synonyms the Bible uses for this word? _____

_____

_____

2. What motives for reproof are suggested in these verses?

_____

_____

_____

3. In these verses, find examples of ways reproof is received.

_____

_____

_____

_____

4. What kind of person benefits from advice and reproof?

_____

_____

5. Who is speaking in 1:23-31? Is this passage an example of excommunication attitudes?_____

_____

_____

6. When should reproof be verbal? When corporal or active?

_____

_____

_____

7. Is it wrong to withhold a needed reproof? Support your answer with Scripture._____

_____

_____

8. Who should be reproved? Cite examples from these verses. _____

_____

_____

9. What are the results for those who fail to heed advice or reproof? _____

_____

_____

10. What happens to those who refuse God's reproof? _____

_____

_____

MORE LIGHT FROM THE BIBLE

11. Are a scoffer and a simple man the same (19:25; 21:11)? Why is reproof ineffective for scoffers? Compare these

verses with Matthew 7:6. _____

_____

_____

_____

12. Reproof presupposes judgment. What advice on this matter do we find in Matthew 7:1-5? _____

_____

_____

13. Who may reprove others or advise them? May younger people reprove older people? See 1 Timothy 5:1. _____

_____

_____

14. What practical advice on the art of reproving is given in Matthew 18:15-17? _____

_____

_____

15. Find some biblical examples of people giving and receiving advice or reproof. _____

_____

_____

_____

LIGHT FOR OUR LIVES

16. What are the attributes of a good reprover? _____

_____

17. By whose standards is one to judge an action worthy of reproof? _____

_____

_____

18. Should Christians reprove unbelieving neighbors for sabbath violations? _____

_____

19. Should one reprove a person who has taken God's name in vain? If so, how? _____

_____

_____

20. Should a person be reproved before he presents his defense? _____

_____

_____

21. Is public or private reproof more effective? _____

_____

_____

22. If the reproved refuses to listen, is the reprover free of responsibility to that person? Is he to feel hurt or vengeful because his rebuke or advice was ignored? _____

_____

_____

23. Should a Christian always be tolerant and say, "Live and

let live"? _____

_____

_____

_____

24. Where should God's people go for advice and help? __

_____

_____

7

NEIGHBORS

"Say not unto thy neighbor, Go, and come again, and tomorrow I will give; when thou hast it by thee. Devise not evil against thy neighbor, seeing he dwelleth securely by thee" (Proverbs 3:28,29).

"Can one go upon hot coals, and his feet not be burned? So he that goeth in to his neighbor's wife; whosoever toucheth her shall not be innocent" (6:28-29).

"A hypocrite with his mouth destroyeth his neighbor: but through knowledge shall the just be delivered. . . . He that is void of wisdom despiseth his neighbor: but a man of understanding holdeth his peace" (11:9,12).

"The righteous is more excellent than his neighbor: but the way of the wicked seduceth them" (12:26).

"The poor is hated even of his own neighbor: but the rich hath many friends. He that despiseth his neighbor sinneth: but he that hath mercy on the poor, happy is he" (14:20,21).

"A violent man enticeth his neighbor, and leadeth him into the way that is not good" (16:29).

"He that is first in his own cause seemeth just; but his neighbor cometh and searcheth him" (18:17).

"Wealth maketh many friends; but the poor is separated from his neighbor" (19:4).

"The soul of the wicked desireth evil: his neighbor findeth no favor in his eyes" (21:10).

"Be not a witness against thy neighbor without cause; and deceive not with thy lips. Say not, I will do so to him as he hath done to me: I will render to the man according to his work" (24:28,29).

"Go not forth hastily to strive, lest thou know not what to do in the end thereof, when thy neighbor hath put thee to shame. Debate thy cause with thy neighbor himself; and discover not a secret to another: Lest he that heareth it put thee to shame, and thine infamy turn not away. . . . Withdraw thy foot from thy neighbor's house; lest he be weary of thee, and so hate thee. A man that beareth false witness against his neighbor is a maul, and a sword, and a sharp arrow" (25:8-10,17,18).

"As a mad man who casteth firebrands, arrows, and death, So is the man that deceiveth his neighbor, and saith, Am not I in sport? (26:18-19).

"Thine own friend, and thy father's friend, forsake not; neither go into thy brother's house in the day of thy calamity: for better is a neighbor that is near than a brother far off" (27:10).

"A man that flattereth his neighbor spreadeth a net for his feet" (29:5).

RELATED VERSES FROM PROVERBS

"If thou forbear to deliver them that are drawn unto death, and those that are ready to be slain; If thou sayest, Behold, we knew it not; doth not he that pondereth the heart consider it?" (24:11-12).

"If thine enemy be hungry, give him bread to eat; and if he be thirsty, give him water to drink: For thou shalt heap coals of fire upon his head, and the Lord shall reward thee" (25:21-22).

"He that passeth by, and meddleth with strife belonging not to him, is like one that taketh a dog by the ears" (26:17).

"He that giveth unto the poor shall not lack: but he that hideth his eyes shall have many a curse" (28:27).

CASTING LIGHT ON THESE VERSES

1. According to these verses, who is my neighbor? _____

_____

_____

Does this agree with Jesus' answer in Luke 10:29-37?

_____

2. What is my responsibility to my neighbor? What factors enter in as shown in the verses below? _____

_____

_____

_____

3. Does Proverbs 12:26 teach an attitude of pride or self-

righteousness? (Be sure to read this verse in other Bible translations.) _____

_____

_____

4. Why is the poor neighbor hated (14:20)? What does Jesus teach about this in Luke 14:12-14? _____

_____

_____

_____

5. Explain 18:17 as thoroughly as you can. In connection with this verse, discuss this question: Does our devotion to religion win or repel neighbors? _____

_____

_____

6. Which of these verses is related to the "Golden Rule" (Matt. 7:12)? _____

_____

7. What does 25:8-10 teach about settling neighborhood problems? _____

_____

_____

8. According to these verses, how involved should one become with his neighbor? What dangers may be encountered in this involvement?_____

_____

_____

_____

9. Can you give an example of 26:18-19? _____

_____

_____

10. Compare Proverbs 29:5 with Ephesians 4:25. _____

_____

_____

MORE LIGHT FROM THE BIBLE

11. What facets of neighborliness do the following verses illustrate?

    Exodus 22:7-8 _____

    Leviticus 25:14 _____

    Deuteronomy 19:14 _____

    23:24 _____

    Ecclesiastes 4:4 _____

    Jeremiah 22:13 _____

    Luke 1:58 _____

    15:6,9 _____

12. What do Leviticus 19:18; Mark 12:33; Luke 10:27; Romans 13:9-10; Galatians 5:14; and James 2:8 have in common?_____

_____

_____

LIGHT FOR OUR LIVES

13. Can a person adequately love his neighbor if he does not love himself?_____

_____

_____

14. In what ways does a person's (or family's) daily life in the neighborhood enhance or destroy his witness for Christ?

_____

_____

15. What are some ways in which a person can actively show love for his neighbor? _____

_____

_____

16. The news media inform us of the problems of the whole world. Is the whole world our neighborhood now? Explain. (See related verses above.) _____

_____

_____

_____

8

WORK AND LAZINESS

"My son, attend unto my wisdom, and bow thine ear to my understanding:
. . . Remove thy way far from her [the strange woman], . . . Lest strangers be
filled with thy wealth; and thy labors be in the house of a stranger" (Proverbs
5:1,8a,10).

"Go to the ant, thou sluggard; consider her ways, and be wise: Which
having no guide, overseer, or ruler, Provideth her meat in the summer, and
gathereth her food in the harvest. How long wilt thou sleep, O sluggard?
when wilt thou arise out of thy sleep? Yet a little sleep, a little slumber, a little
folding of the hands to sleep: So shall thy poverty come as one that travelleth,
and thy want as an armed man" (6:6-11).

"He becometh poor that dealeth with a slack hand: but the hand of the
diligent maketh rich. He that gathereth in summer is a wise son: but he that
sleepeth in harvest is a son that causeth shame. . . . The labor of the righteous
tendeth to life: the fruit of the wicked to sin. . . . As vinegar to the teeth, and as
smoke to the eyes, so is the sluggard to them that send him" (10:4,5,16,26).

"He that tilleth his land shall be satisfied with bread: but he that followeth
vain persons is void of understanding. . . . A man shall be satisfied with good
by the fruit of his mouth: and the recompense of a man's hands shall be
rendered unto him. . . . The hand of the diligent shall bear rule: but the
slothful shall be under tribute. . . . The slothful man roasteth not that which
he took in hunting: but the substance of a diligent man is precious"
(12:11,14,24,27).

"The soul of the sluggard desireth, and hath nothing: but the soul of the
diligent shall be made fat. . . . Wealth gotten by vanity shall be diminished:
but he that gathereth by labor shall increase. . . . Much food is in the tillage of
the poor: but there is that is destroyed for want of judgment" (13:4,11,23).

"Where no oxen are, the crib is clean: but much increase is by the strength
of the ox. . . . In all labor there is profit: but the talk of the lips tendeth only to
penury" (14:4,23).

"The way of the slothful man is as a hedge of thorns: but the way of the righteous is made plain" (15:19).

"Commit thy works unto the LORD, and thy thoughts shall be established. . . . He that laboreth laboreth for himself; for his mouth craveth it of him" (16:3,26).

"He also that is slothful in his work is brother to him that is a great waster" (18:9).

"Slothfulness casteth into a deep sleep; and an idle soul shall suffer hunger. . . . A slothful man hideth his hand in his bosom, and will not so much as bring it to his mouth again" (19:15,24).

"The sluggard will not plow by reason of the cold; therefore shall he beg in harvest, and have nothing. . . . Even a child is known by his doings, whether his work be pure, and whether it be right. . . . Love not sleep, lest thou come to poverty; open thine eyes, and thou shalt be satisfied with bread. . . . Bread of deceit is sweet to a man; but afterwards his mouth shall be filled with gravel" (20:4,11,13,17).

"The thoughts of the diligent tend only to plenteousness; but of every one that is hasty only to want. . . . The way of man is froward and strange: but as for the pure, his work is right. . . . The desire of the slothful killeth him; for his hands refuse to labor. He coveteth greedily all the day long: but the righteous giveth and spareth not" (21:5,8,25-26).

"The slothful man saith, There is a lion without, I shall be slain in the streets. . . . Seest thou a man diligent in his business? he shall stand before kings; he shall not stand before mean men" (22:13,29).

"Labor not to be rich: cease from thine own wisdom. . . . For the drunkard and the glutton shall come to poverty: and drowsiness shall clothe a man with rags" (23:4,21).

"Prepare thy work without, and make it fit for thyself in the field; and afterwards build thine house. . . . I went by the field of the slothful, and by the vineyard of the man void of understanding; And lo, it was all grown over with thorns, and nettles had covered the face thereof, and the stone wall thereof was broken down. Then I saw, and considered it well: I looked upon it, and received instruction. Yet a little sleep, a little folding of the hands to sleep: So shall thy poverty come as one that travelleth; and thy want as an armed man" (24:27,30-34).

"The slothful man saith, There is a lion in the way; a lion is in the streets. As the door turneth upon his hinges, so doth the slothful upon his bed. The slothful hideth his hand in his bosom; it grieveth him to bring it again to his mouth. The sluggard is wiser in his own conceit than seven men that can render a reason" (26:13-16).

"Whoso keepeth the fig tree shall eat the fruit thereof: so he that waiteth on his master shall be honored. . . . Be thou diligent to know the state of thy flocks, and look well to thy herds. For riches are not for ever: and doth the crown endure to every generation? The hay appeareth, and the tender grass sheweth itself, and herbs of the mountains are gathered. The lambs are for thy clothing, and the goats are the price of the field. And thou shalt have goats' milk enough for thy food, for the food of thy household, and for the maintenance for thy maidens" (27:18,23-27).

"He that tilleth his land shall have plenty of bread: but he that followeth after vain persons shall have poverty enough. A faithful man shall abound with blessings: but he that maketh haste to be rich shall not be innocent. . . . He that hasteth to be rich hath an evil eye, and considereth not that poverty shall come upon him" (28:19,20,22).

"There be four things which are little upon the earth, but they are exceeding wise: The ants are a people not strong, yet they prepare their meat in the summer; The conies are but a feeble folk, yet they make their houses in the rocks; The locusts have no king, yet go they forth all of them by bands; The spider taketh hold with her hands, and is in kings' palaces" (30:24-28).

"Who can find a virtuous woman? for her price is far above rubies. . . . She seeketh wool, and flax, and worketh willingly with her hands. She is like the merchants' ships; she bringeth her food from afar. She riseth also while it is yet night, and giveth meat to her household, and a portion to her maidens. She considereth a field, and buyeth it: with the fruit of her hands she planteth a vineyard. She girdeth her loins with strength, and strengtheneth her arms. She perceiveth that her merchandise is good: her candle goeth not out by night. She layeth her hands to the spindle, and her hands hold the distaff. She stretcheth out her hand to the poor; yea, she reacheth forth her hands to the needy. She is not afraid of the snow for her household: for all her household are clothed with scarlet. She maketh herself coverings of tapestry; her clothing is silk and purple. . . . She maketh fine linen, and selleth it; and delivereth girdles unto the merchant. . . . She looketh well to the ways of her household, and eateth not the bread of idleness. . . . Give her of the fruit of her hands; and let her own works praise her in the gates" (31:10,13-22,24,27,31).

CASTING LIGHT ON THESE VERSES

1. What descriptive words are used in these verses to paint a portrait of a good worker? _____

_____

_____

Which words are used to describe the lazy person? ___

_____

_____

2. What motives for work are suggested? _____

_____

_____

_____

3. What good and bad attitudes toward work do we find in
   these verses?_____

   _____

   _____

   _____

   _____

4. What can animals teach us about work? See 6:6-8;
   30:24-28. _____

   _____

   _____

5. Explain 6:11 and 24:34._____

   _____

   _____

6. What is meant by a "slack hand" in 10:4?_____

   _____

7. Why are smoke and vinegar referred to in 10:26? What do
   these examples tell us about the feelings of the sender?

   _____

   _____

   _____

8. Many successful businessmen are leaders in civic affairs and politics (see 12:24; 22:29). Do these proverbs endorse the "American dream" that even the poorest man can succeed and climb to the top of the social scale through hard work? _____

_____

_____

9. What does 12:27 mean?_____

_____

10. How can 13:4 be applied to spiritual matters?_____

_____

11. Read 13:23 in other versions. How is this true today in parts of the world?_____

_____

_____

12. What does 14:4 suggest about the equipment of a good worker? _____

_____

13. What is meant by "the way" in 15:19 and 21:8? Check other versions. _____

_____

14. How can 18:9 apply to use of food and natural resources?

_____

_____

15. Read 20:17 in other versions. How can this truth be applied to dishonesty and stealing in today's work world? Compare this verse with 28:20,22._____

_____

_____

16. Did the early pioneers in America follow the advice in 24:27? Did it prove to be good advice? How can it apply to us today?_____

_____

_____

17. Discuss the vivid and humorous picture of the slothful man in 26:13-16. Why does he say "a lion is in the streets"? How is he like a door turning on its hinges? Read 26:15 in other versions. Have you found 26:16 to be true?

_____

_____

_____

_____

18. What does 27:18 say about fair wages? Why are profit-sharing plans and prizes and contests successful motivators for employees? _____

_____

_____

19. In 12:11 and 28:19 we read about following after "vain persons." What are contemporary examples of this?____

_____

_____

20. In the verses selected from chapter 31, we find an example of the ideal woman whose life is the embodiment of the advice presented in our lesson. Why was a woman chosen to portray this ideal? _____

_____

_____

MORE LIGHT FROM THE BIBLE

21. What do we know about God's work? See Genesis 2:2; Deuteronomy 32:4; Psalms 8:3; 104:24; John 5:17; 6:28-29; 9:4. _____

_____

_____

22. What does the Bible say about wages? See Leviticus 19:13; Luke 3:14; 10:7; 1 Corinthians 3:8; Galatians 6:6; 2 Thessalonians 3:10-12; 1 Timothy 5:17-18; 2 Timothy 2:6. _____

_____

_____

_____

_____

23. What does the Bible say about God's recognition of our work? See Hebrews 6:10 and Revelation 2:2. _____

_____

24. Is work a necessary evil, part of the curse for sin? See Genesis 1–3. _____

_____

_____

25. What can we learn about work from these verses: Ecclesiastes 5:18-20; 9:10; Nehemiah 2:18; 4:6; John 9:4; 1 Thessalonians 4:10-12? _____

_____

_____

_____

_____

26. Why did Jesus not extol the work of the elder brother in Luke 15:25-32? _____

_____

_____

27. Note the blessings in Ecclesiastes 5:12; Matthew 11:28; Revelation 14:13. _____

_____

_____

28. Read the following passages, which tell about the work of some Bible characters: Exodus 2:9; 2 Chronicles 15:1-8; 31:20-21; 34:8-13; Romans 16:1-2,6,12,21. _____

_____

_____

_____

_____

LIGHT FOR OUR LIVES

29. Are some careers or jobs more honorable than others?

_____

_____

30. Do leisure time and a shorter work week foster laziness?

_____

_____

31. Do welfare programs foster laziness? _____

_____

_____

32. If a child seems to be lazy, what can be done about it?

_____

_____

33. Why does work sometimes seem like drudgery? _____

_____

_____

34. How can we find more joy in work? _____

_____

_____

35. Are labor unions and strikes compatible with the Bible's teaching about work? _____

_____

_____

9

CHILD TRAINING

"My son, hear the instruction of thy father, and forsake not the law of thy mother: For they shall be an ornament of grace unto thy head, and chains about thy neck" (Proverbs 1:8-9).

"My son, if thou wilt receive my words, and hide my commandments with thee; So that thou incline thine ear unto wisdom, and apply thine heart to understanding; Yea, if thou criest after knowledge, and liftest up thy voice for understanding; If thou seekest her as silver, and searchest for her as for hid treasures; Then shalt thou understand the fear of the Lord, and find the knowledge of God" (2:1-5).

Chapters 3–7 are a loving letter from a father to a son. Some excerpts from this letter follow.

"My son, forget not my law; but let thine heart keep my commandments: . . . Trust in the Lord with all thine heart; and lean not unto thine own understanding. In all thy ways acknowledge him, and he shall direct thy paths. . . . My son, despise not the chastening of the Lord; neither be weary of his correction: For whom the Lord loveth he correcteth; even as a father the son in whom he delighteth" (3:1,5-6,11-12).

"Hear, ye children, the instruction of a father, and attend to know understanding. For I give you good doctrine, forsake ye not my law. For I was my father's son, tender and only beloved in the sight of my mother. He taught me also, and said unto me, Let thine heart retain my words: keep my commandments, and live. Get wisdom, get understanding: forget it not; neither decline from the words of my mouth. . . . Hear, O my son, and receive my sayings; and the years of thy life shall be many. I have taught thee in the way of wisdom; I have led thee in right paths. . . . My son, attend to my words; . . . Let them not depart from thine eyes; keep them in the midst of thine heart. For they are life unto those that find them, and health to all their flesh. Keep thy heart with all diligence; for out of it are the issues of life. Put away from thee a froward mouth, and perverse lips put far from thee. Let thine eyes look right on, and let thine eyelids look straight before thee. Ponder the path of thy feet, and let all thy ways be established. Turn not to the right hand nor to the left: remove thy foot from evil" (4:1-5,10-11,20-27).

"My son, attend unto my wisdom, and bow thine ear to my understanding: That thou mayest regard discretion, and that thy lips may keep knowledge" (5:1-2).

"My son, keep thy father's commandment, and forsake not the law of thy mother: Bind them continually upon thine heart, and tie them about thy neck. When thou goest, it shall lead thee; when thou sleepest, it shall keep thee; and when thou awakest, it shall talk with thee. For the commandment is a lamp; and the law is light; and reproofs of instruction are the way of life" (6:20-23).

"My son, keep my words, and lay up my commandments with thee. Keep my commandments, and live; and my law as the apple of thine eye. Bind them upon thy fingers, write them upon the table of thine heart" (7:1-3).

"Now therefore hearken unto me, O ye children: for blessed are they that keep my ways. Hear instruction, and be wise, and refuse it not" (8:32,33).

"The proverbs of Solomon. A wise son maketh a glad father: but a foolish son is the heaviness of his mother. . . . He that gathereth in summer is a wise son: but he that sleepeth in harvest is a son that causeth shame" (10:1,5).

"A wise son heareth his father's instruction: but a scorner heareth not rebuke. . . . A good man leaveth an inheritance to his children's children: and the wealth of the sinner is laid up for the just. . . . He that spareth his rod hateth his son: but he that loveth him chasteneth him betimes" (13:1,22,24).

"A wise servant shall have rule over a son that causeth shame, and shall have part of the inheritance among the brethren. . . . Children's children are the crown of old men; and the glory of children are their fathers. . . . He that begetteth a fool doeth it to his sorrow: and the father of a fool hath no joy. . . . A foolish son is a grief to his father, and bitterness to her that bare him" (17:2,6,21,25).

"A foolish son is the calamity of his father: and the contentions of a wife are a continual dropping. . . . Chasten thy son while there is hope, and let not thy soul spare for his crying. . . . He that wasteth his father, and chaseth away his mother, is a son that causeth shame, and bringeth reproach. Cease, my son, to hear the instruction that causeth to err from the words of knowledge" (19:13,18,26,27).

"The just man walketh in his integrity: his children are blessed after him. . . . Even a child is known by his doings, whether his work be pure, and whether it be right. . . . Whoso curseth his father or his mother, his lamp shall be put out in obscure darkness" (20:7,11,20).

"Train up a child in the way he should go: and when he is old, he will not depart from it. . . . Foolishness is bound in the heart of a child; but the rod of correction shall drive it far from him" (22:6,15).

"Withhold not correction from the child: for if thou beatest him with the rod, he shall not die. Thou shalt beat him with the rod, and shalt deliver his soul from hell. My son, if thine heart be wise, my heart shall rejoice, even mine. Yea, my reins shall rejoice, when thy lips speak right things. Let not thine heart envy sinners: but be thou in the fear of the Lord all the day long. For surely there is an end; and thine expectation shall not be cut off. Hear thou, my son, and be wise, and guide thine heart in the way. Be not among winebibbers; among riotous eaters of flesh: For the drunkard and the glutton shall come to poverty: and drowsiness shall clothe a man with rags. Hearken unto thy father that begat thee, and despise not thy mother when she is old. Buy the truth, and sell it not; also wisdom, and instruction, and understanding. The father of the righteous shall greatly rejoice: and he that begetteth a wise child shall have joy of him. Thy father and thy mother shall be glad, and she that bare thee shall rejoice. My son, give me thine heart, and let thine eyes observe my ways" (23:13-26).

"My son, fear the Lord and the king: and meddle not with them that are given to change: For their calamity shall rise suddenly; and who knoweth the ruin of them both?" (24:21-22).

"My son, be wise, and make my heart glad, that I may answer him that reproacheth me" (27:11).

"Whoso keepeth the law is a wise son: but he that is a companion of riotous men shameth his father. . . . Whoso robbeth his father or his mother, and saith, It is no transgression; the same is the companion of a destroyer" (28:7,24).

"Whoso loveth wisdom rejoiceth his father: but he that keepeth company with harlots spendeth his substance. . . . The rod and reproof give wisdom: but a child left to himself bringeth his mother to shame. . . . Correct thy son, and he shall give thee rest; yea, he shall give delight unto thy soul. . . . He that delicately bringeth up his servant from a child shall have him become his son at the length" (29:3,15,17,21).

"There is a generation that curseth their father, and doth not bless their mother. . . . The eye that mocketh at his father, and despiseth to obey his mother, the ravens of the valley shall pick it out, and the young eagles shall eat it" (30:11,17).

Chapter 31 is a mother's advice to her son. Some excerpts from this chapter follow.

"[The virtuous woman] . . . openeth her mouth with wisdom; and in her tongue is the law of kindness. . . . Her children arise up, and call her blessed: her husband also, and he praiseth her" (31:26,28).

CASTING LIGHT ON THESE VERSES

1. How are the teachings of parents like ornaments or necklaces for their children (1:8-9)? _____

2. The words *hearken, listen, attend,* and *give ear* are found throughout these verses from Proverbs. Underline all the references to *hearing* which you find in these verses. How many did you find? _____

   In the prophecy of Isaiah, God the Father speaks of Israel as His children (Isa. 1:2-3). Notice the tone of Isaiah 1 and the references to listening in chapters 1 and 48–52. Why is it necessary for a parent to tell a child to listen so many times? _____

   _____

   _____

3. The entire Book of Proverbs is intended to be a guide for youth. It treats every aspect of life. The first two chapters deal with the importance of wisdom. Chapters 3–7 contain a wealth of practical advice.

   a. What is the "tone" of the instruction given in these chapters? _____

   _____

   b. What does chapter 7 have to say to daughters? _____

   _____

   _____

4. Notice the frank, direct discussion of problems and temptations. What guidelines for sex education can you glean from these verses? _____

   _____

   _____

5. What kind of inheritance is meant in 13:22? _____

_____

_____

6. Give a practical example of 17:2. What is implied here?

_____

_____

7. When children are foolish and cause grief, is it always the fault of the parents (17:21,25)? How can parents handle their disappointments and frustrations in dealing with an unresponsive child?_____

_____

_____

_____

8. Is there a relationship between a contentious wife and a foolish son as a source of grief for a man (19:13)? ____

_____

9. Do 19:18 and other verses like it (22:15; 23:13,14) endorse cruelty to children?_____

_____

10. Should parents let their children "walk on them" or misuse them (19:26)? _____

_____

11. Should parents take "backtalk" from their children (20:20)?_____

_____

12. Companions also mold a child (28:7). How can parents encourage children to choose proper companions? What can parents do when children choose improper companions?_____

_____

_____

_____

13. What is meant or implied by "left to himself" in 29:15?

_____

_____

14. According to chapter 31, what values should a mother teach her children to look for in a prospective mate?

_____

_____

_____

15. Do these selections from Proverbs suggest that a father has more responsibility than a mother in the training of a child?_____

_____

_____

MORE LIGHT FROM THE BIBLE

16. What do the following passages tell us about child training?
    a. Genesis 18:17-19 _____

    _____

b. Deuteronomy 6:4-9,20-25 _____

_____

_____

c. Deuteronomy 21:18-21 _____

_____

_____

d. Judges 13:8 _____

_____

e. Psalm 78:1-8 _____

_____

f. Psalm 103:13-14 _____

_____

g. 1 Corinthians 13:11 _____

_____

h. Ephesians 6:1-4 _____

_____

17. Find illustrations in the Bible of the results of good or bad
child training. _____

_____

_____

_____

_____

LIGHT FOR OUR LIVES

18. a. If the school is an extension of the home, do teachers have the same control, privileges, and responsibilities for the children that their parents have? _____

_____

_____

b. Who should discipline children—parents or teachers?

_____

c. What types of discipline do you feel teachers should give? _____

_____

d. How can parents and teachers work together more effectively? _____

_____

_____

e. Can you give any examples of special wisdom or blessing in the handling of school discipline problems?

_____

_____

19. What is our responsibility to neighbor children? _____

_____

_____

20. What is the role of grandparents in child training? _____

_____

_____

21. Where should we go for help in problems that evolve in child training?_____

_____

_____

22. What are the rewards for faithful child training?_____

_____

_____

10

FEAR AND FEAR OF THE LORD

"The fear of the LORD is the beginning of knowledge: but fools despise wisdom and instruction. . . . Because I have called, and ye refused; I have stretched out my hand, and no man regarded; But ye have set at nought all my counsel, and would none of my reproof: I also will laugh at your calamity; I will mock when your fear cometh; When your fear cometh as desolation, and your destruction cometh as a whirlwind; when distress and anguish cometh upon you. Then shall they call upon me, but I will not answer; they shall seek me early, but they shall not find me: For that they hated knowledge, and did not choose the fear of the LORD: . . . But whoso hearkeneth unto me shall dwell safely, and shall be quiet from fear of evil" (Proverbs 1:7,24-29,33).

"My son, if thou wilt receive my words, and hide my commandments with thee; So that thou incline thine ear unto wisdom, and apply thine heart to understanding; Yea, if thou criest after knowledge, and liftest up thy voice for understanding; If thou seekest her as silver, and searchest for her as for hid treasures; Then shalt thou understand the fear of the LORD, and find the knowledge of God" (2:1-5).

"Be not wise in thine own eyes: fear the LORD, and depart from evil. It shall be health to thy navel, and marrow to thy bones. . . . When thou liest down, thou shalt not be afraid: yea, thou shalt lie down, and thy sleep shall be sweet. Be not afraid of sudden fear, neither of the desolation of the wicked, when it cometh. For the LORD shall be thy confidence, and shall keep thy foot from being taken" (3:7-8,24-26).

"The fear of the LORD is to hate evil: pride, and arrogancy, and the evil way, and the froward mouth, do I hate" (8:13).

"The fear of the LORD is the beginning of wisdom: and the knowledge of the holy is understanding" (9:10).

"The fear of the wicked, it shall come upon him: but the desire of the righteous shall be granted. . . . The fear of the LORD prolongeth days:

but the years of the wicked shall be shortened" (10:24,27).

"Whoso despiseth the word shall be destroyed: but he that feareth the commandment shall be rewarded" (13:13).

"He that walketh in his uprightness feareth the Lord: but he that is perverse in his ways despiseth him. . . . In the fear of the Lord is strong confidence: and his children shall have a place of refuge. The fear of the Lord is a fountain of life, to depart from the snares of death" (14:2,26,27).

"Better is a little with the fear of the Lord than great treasure and trouble therewith. . . . The fear of the Lord is the instruction of wisdom; and before honor is humility" (15:16,33).

"By mercy and truth iniquity is purged: and by the fear of the Lord men depart from evil" (16:6).

"The fear of the Lord tendeth to life: and he that hath it shall abide satisfied; he shall not be visited with evil" (19:23).

"The fear of a king is as the roaring of a lion: whoso provoketh him to anger sinneth against his own soul" (20:2).

"By humility and the fear of the Lord are riches, and honor, and life" (22:4).

"Let not thine heart envy sinners: but be thou in the fear of the Lord all the day long" (23:17).

"My son, fear thou the Lord and the king: and meddle not with them that are given to change" (24:21).

"Happy is the man that feareth alway: but he that hardeneth his heart shall fall into mischief" (28:14).

"The fear of man bringeth a snare: but whoso putteth his trust in the Lord shall be safe" (29:25).

"Favor is deceitful, and beauty is vain: but a woman that feareth the Lord, she shall be praised" (31:30).

CASTING LIGHT ON THESE VERSES

1. What is fear? What are some synonyms for fear? _____

_____

_____

2. What is fear of the Lord? _____

_____

_____

3. Does fear inspire hate or love? _____

_____

4. After studying these verses, complete this sentence: "The fear of the Lord *is*. . . ." _____

_____

_____

5. After studying these verses, complete this sentence: "The fear of the Lord *gives*. . . ." _____

_____

_____

6. According to the verses from chapter 1, under what circumstances does God withhold His help in fearful situations? _____

_____

_____

7. How are fear of the Lord and fear of a king alike (20:2; 24:21)? _____

_____

8. Read 28:14 in other Bible versions. _____

_____

_____

9. Why is the woman who fears the Lord worthy of praise (31:30)? _____

_____

_____

MORE LIGHT FROM THE BIBLE

10. Was man created having fear? See Genesis 3. _____

_____

_____

11. Can you cite any examples from the Bible in which people were afraid? _____

_____

_____

_____

_____

12. According to the Bible, what should we fear?_____

_____

_____

_____

13. According to the Bible, what should we not fear? (You will find help in answering these questions if you look up the Bible verses listed under "fear" or "fear not" in a Bible concordance.)_____

_____

_____

_____

14. How many biblical "fear nots" (or similar words) can you find? _____

_____

LIGHT FOR OUR LIVES

15. Is fear ever good for us? _____
_____
_____
_____

16. Who has more fear—young or old people? Why? _____
_____
_____

17. What things do you fear? _____
_____
_____

18. Is it wrong for a Christian to be fearful? _____
_____
_____

19. How can children's fears be dealt with? _____
_____
_____

20. What Bible verses comfort you? _____
_____
_____

11

FRIENDS

"My son, if thou be surety for thy friend, if thou hast stricken thy hand with a stranger, Thou art snared with the words of thy mouth, thou art taken with the words of thy mouth. Do this now, my son, and deliver thyself, when thou art come into the hand of thy friend; go, humble thyself, and make sure thy friend" (Proverbs 6:1-3).

"The poor is hated even of his own neighbor: but the rich hath many friends" (14:20).

"A froward man soweth strife: and a whisperer separateth chief friends" (16:28).

"He that covereth a transgression seeketh love; but he that repeateth a matter separateth very friends. . . . A friend loveth at all times, and a brother is born for adversity. A man void of understanding striketh hands, and becometh surety in the presence of his friend" (17:9,17,18).

"A man that hath friends must show himself friendly: and there is a friend that sticketh closer than a brother" (18:24).

"Wealth maketh many friends; but the poor is separated from his neighbor. . . . Many will entreat the favor of the prince: and every man is a friend to him that giveth gifts. All the brethren of the poor do hate him: how much more do his friends go far from him? he pursueth them with words, yet they are wanting to him" (19:4,6,7).

"He that loveth pureness of heart, for the grace of his lips the king shall be his friend. . . . Make no friendship with an angry man; and with a furious man thou shalt not go: Lest thou learn his ways, and get a snare to thy soul" (22:11,24-25).

"Faithful are the wounds of a friend; but the kisses of an enemy are deceitful. . . . Ointment and perfume rejoice the heart: so doth the sweetness of a man's friend by hearty counsel. Thine own friend, and thy father's friend, forsake not; neither go into thy brother's house in the day of thy calamity: for better is a neighbor that is near than a brother far off. . . . He that blesseth his friend with a loud voice, rising early in the morning, it shall be counted a curse to him. . . . Iron sharpeneth iron; so a man sharpeneth the countenance of his friend'' (27:6,9,10,14,17).

CASTING LIGHT ON THESE VERSES

1. a. Why do the rich have many friends (14:20; 19:4,6,7)?

   _____

   b. Are people who like us because of what we have true friends?_____

   _____

   _____

2. Compare 14:20; 19:4,6,7, and 17:17. What quality of true friendship is cited in 17:17?_____

   _____

3. How can friends be more effective than relatives in times of trouble (27:10)? _____

   _____

   _____

4. a. What does 18:24 (KJV) tell us about winning and keeping friends? _____

   _____

   b. Read this verse in other versions. What further insights on friendship did you gain? _____

   _____

   _____

   c. Can you illustrate this truth from your life? _____

_____

_____

d. Does the last half of this verse refer to Christ?_____

_____

5. What is meant by "covering a transgression" (17:9)? Does this imply that we are to protect our friends from just punishment? _____

_____

_____

_____

6. a. What does it mean to be "surety" for someone? ___

_____

b. What does it mean to "strike hands" with someone?

_____

c. What is the difference between being surety for a friend and "making sure" your friend?_____

_____

_____

d. Would "being surety" be a part of a Christian's witness, like "going the extra mile" (Matt. 5:41)? _____

_____

7. Read 17:18 in other versions. Does this express the same advice as given in 6:1-3? _____

_____

_____

8. How can a gossip or a whisperer break up friendships (16:28)? Why would someone want to do this? _____

_____

_____

_____

9. a. Is it generally true that rulers choose friends who are morally pure and who have the gift of speaking graciously (22:11)?_____

_____

   b. Compare 22:11 with Matthew 5:8 and John 15:14. What conclusion can you draw from this comparison?

_____

_____

10. The NIV translates 22:24, "Do not make friends with a hot-tempered man, do not associate with one easily angered." Why would a hot-tempered man be a bad friend? _____

_____

_____

11. Iron can be used as a tool. How can a person be like iron, shaping or sculpting his friend (27:17)? _____

_____

12. Give examples of "faithful are the wounds of a friend" and "kisses of an enemy are deceitful" (27:6). _____

_____

_____

13. How is a friend's advice like ointment and perfume (27:9)? _____

_____

_____

14. Give an example of 27:14. _____

_____

_____

MORE LIGHT FROM THE BIBLE

15. Look up the following references and list the elements or facets of friendship that you discover:
    a. 2 Chronicles 20:7; Genesis 18:17; Isaiah 41:8; James 2:23 _____

    _____

    _____

    b. Exodus 33:11 _____

    _____

    c. 1 Samuel 19–20 (especially 20:17); 2 Samuel 9____

    _____

    _____

    d. Job 2:11_____

    _____

e. Luke 7:6 _____

_____

f. Luke 11:5-8 _____

_____

g. Luke 15:9 _____

_____

h. Luke 23:12 _____

_____

i. Acts 10:24,44-48 _____

_____

j. Acts 19:29-31 _____

_____

k. Acts 27:1-3 _____

_____

16. Betrayal by friends is a bitter experience. Read about it in these passages: Job 16:20; 19:14-22; Psalms 38:9-11; 41:9; Matthew 26:48-50,56; 2 Timothy 4:14-17. Write out your thoughts. _____

_____

_____

_____

17. What does Jesus ask of His friends (John 15:12-17)? ____

_____

_____

18. How does He express His friendship in these verses from John 15? _____

_____

_____

LIGHT FOR OUR LIVES

19. Where should we go to look for friends?_____

_____

_____

20. What qualities should we look for in friends?_____

_____

_____

_____

21. What responsibilities does friendship involve? _____

_____

_____

22. What should parents do if they do not approve of their children's choice of friends? _____

_____

_____

23. What advice can we give a child who says he has no friends? _____

_____

_____

24. How is Jesus the perfect Friend? _____

_____

_____

_____

25. How is your life, as a friend of Jesus, different from the life of someone who does not know Him as Lord and Savior?

_____

_____

_____

12

GOALS AND TREASURES

"My son, if thou wilt receive my words, and hide my commandments with thee; So that thou incline thine ear unto wisdom and apply thine heart to understanding; Yea, if thou criest after knowledge, and liftest up thy voice for understanding; If thou seekest her as silver, and searchest for her as for hid treasures; Then shalt thou understand the fear of the Lord, and find the knowledge of God. For the Lord giveth wisdom: out of his mouth cometh knowledge and understanding" (Proverbs 2:1-6).

"Happy is the man that findeth wisdom, and the man thet getteth understanding. For the merchandise of it is better than the merchandise of silver, and the gain thereof than fine gold. She is more precious than rubies: and all the things thou canst desire are not to be compared unto her. Length of days is in her right hand; and in her left hand riches and honor. Her ways are ways of pleasantness, and all her paths are peace. She is a tree of life to them that lay hold upon her: and happy is everyone that retaineth her. . . . The wise shall inherit glory: but shame shall be the promotion of fools" (3:13-18,35).

"Wisdom is the principal thing; therefore get wisdom: and with all thy getting get understanding. Exalt her, and she shall promote thee: she shall bring thee to honor, when thou dost embrace her. She shall give to thine head an ornament of grace: a crown of glory shall she deliver to thee" (4:7-9).

"Receive my instruction, and not silver; and knowledge rather than choice gold. For wisdom is better than rubies; and all the things that may be desired are not to be compared to it. I wisdom dwell with prudence, and find out knowledge of witty inventions. . . . Riches and honor are with me; yea, durable riches and righteousness. My fruit is better than gold, yea, than fine gold; and my revenue than choice silver. I lead in the way of righteousness, in the midst of the paths of judgment: That I may cause those that love me to inherit substance; and I will fill their treasures" (8:10-12,18-21).

"Treasures of wickedness profit nothing: but righteousness delivereth from death" (10:2).

"Evil pursueth sinners: but to the righteous good shall be repaid" (13:21).

"In the house of the righteous is much treasure: but in the revenues of the wicked is trouble. . . . Better is a little with the fear of the LORD than great treasure and trouble therewith. Better is a dinner of herbs where love is, than a stalled ox and hatred therewith" (15:6,16-17).

"How much better is it to get wisdom than gold! and to get understanding rather to be chosen than silver!" (16:16).

"There is gold, and a multitude of rubies: but the lips of knowledge are a precious jewel. . . . An inheritance may be gotten hastily at the beginning; but the end thereof shall not be blessed" (20:15,21).

"The getting of treasures by a lying tongue is a vanity tossed to and fro of them that seek death. . . . There is a treasure to be desired and oil in the dwelling of the wise; but a foolish man spendeth it up. He that followeth after righteousness and mercy findeth life, righteousness, and honor" (21:6, 20,21).

"A good name is rather to be chosen than great riches, and loving favor rather than silver and gold" (22:1).

"Through wisdom is a house builded; and by understanding it is established: And by knowledge shall the chambers be filled with all precious and pleasant riches" (24:3-4).

CASTING LIGHT ON THESE VERSES

1. According to these verses, what is the greatest treasure? Do you agree? Why? _____

_____

_____

_____

2. What benefits come with this treasure? _____

_____

_____

_____

3. Do these verses teach that material or nonmaterial riches are more valuable? _____

_____

4. Do these verses denounce material possessions? _____

_____

_____

5. In attaining goals, does the end justify the means?_____

_____

_____

6. How should goals be attained and treasures be obtained?

_____

_____

_____

MORE LIGHT FROM THE BIBLE

7. Evaluate Achan and his deed in the light of these Proverbs. Read Joshua 6:15-21; 7._____

_____

_____

_____

8. Why was Achan put to death?_____

_____

9. What does Hebrews 11:26 say about Moses? See also Matthew 5:11-12. _____

_____

_____

10. What do the buried treasure and the pearl of great price

symbolize in the parables of Jesus (Matt. 13:44-46)? ___

___

11. What is the kingdom of heaven? Are many people aware of its value? Is it necessary to sell all one's possessions to obtain it? ___

___

___

___

___

12. What do we learn in Matthew 6:19-21 about treasures?

___

___

13. What was Paul's goal as expressed in Philippians 3:8-14?

___

___

LIGHT FOR OUR LIVES

14. What are your goals? What are your treasures? ___

___

___

___

15. How can we measure what things are truly valuable to us?

___

___

16. If a child breaks your heirloom dish, or your spouse wrecks your car, how would you handle the matter? What would your handling of this matter indicate about your value system? _____

    _____

    _____

17. If we determine what our goals are, and find them to be unworthy, how should we go about changing them?

    _____

    _____

18. How can we help children choose good goals and treasures? _____

    _____

    _____

    _____

13

WORDS

"Put away from thee a froward mouth, and perverse lips put far from thee" (Proverbs 4:24).

"My son, if thou be surety for thy friend, if thou hast stricken thy hand with a stranger, Thou art snared with the words of thy mouth, thou art taken with the words of thy mouth. . . . A naughty person, a wicked man, walketh with a froward mouth. . . . These six things doth the LORD hate: yea, seven are an abomination unto him: A proud look, a lying tongue, and hands that shed innocent blood, A heart that deviseth wicked imaginations, feet that be swift in running to mischief, A false witness that speaketh lies, and he that soweth discord among brethren. . . . For the commandment is a lamp . . . To keep thee from the evil woman, from the flattery of the tongue of a strange woman" (6:1-2,12,16-19,23a,24).

"Hear; for I will speak of excellent things; and the opening of my lips shall be right things. For my mouth shall speak truth; and wickedness is an abomination to my lips. All the words of my mouth are in righteousness; there is nothing froward or perverse in them. They are all plain to him that understandeth, and right to them that find knowledge. . . . The fear of the LORD is to hate evil: pride, and arrogancy, and the evil way, and the froward mouth, do I hate" (8:6-9,13).

"Blessings are upon the head of the just: but violence covereth the mouth of the wicked. . . . The wise in heart will receive commandments: but a prating fool shall fall. . . . The mouth of a righteous man is a well of life: but violence covereth the mouth of the wicked. . . . In the lips of him that hath understanding wisdom is found: but a rod is for the back of him that is void of understanding. Wise men lay up knowledge: but the mouth of the foolish is near destruction. . . . He that hideth hatred with lying lips, and he that uttereth a slander, is a fool. In the multitude of words there wanteth not sin: but he that refraineth his lips is wise. The tongue of the just is as choice silver: the heart of the wicked is little worth. The lips of the righteous feed many: but fools die for want of wisdom. . . . The mouth of the just bringeth forth wisdom: but the froward tongue shall be cut out. The lips of the righteous know what is acceptable: but the mouth of the wicked speaketh frowardness" (10:6,8,11,13,14,18-21,31,32).

"A hypocrite with his mouth destroyeth his neighbor: but through knowledge shall the just be delivered. . . . By the blessing of the upright the city is exalted: but it is overthrown by the mouth of the wicked. He that is void of wisdom despiseth his neighbor: but a man of understanding holdeth his peace. A talebearer revealeth secrets: but he that is of a faithful spirit concealeth the matter" (11:9,11-13).

"The thoughts of the righteous are right: but the counsels of the wicked are deceit. The words of the wicked are to lie in wait for blood: but the mouth of the upright shall deliver them. . . . The wicked is snared by the transgression of his lips: but the just shall come out of trouble. A man shall be satisfied with good by the fruit of his mouth: and the recompense of a man's hands shall be rendered unto him. . . . A fool's wrath is presently known: but a prudent man covereth shame. He that speaketh truth showeth forth righteousness: but a false witness deceit. There is that speaketh like the piercings of a sword: but the tongue of the wise is health. The lip of truth shall be established for ever: but a lying tongue is but for a moment. . . . Lying lips are abomination to the LORD; but they that deal truly are his delight. . . . Heaviness in the heart of man maketh it stoop: but a good word maketh it glad" (12:5,6,13,14,16-19,22,25).

"A man shall eat good by the fruit of his mouth: but the soul of the transgressors shall eat violence. He that keepeth his mouth keepeth his life: but he that openeth wide his lips shall have destruction. . . . A righteous man hateth lying: but a wicked man is loathsome, and cometh to shame" (13:2,3,5).

"In the mouth of the foolish is a rod of pride: but the lips of the wise shall preserve them. . . . A faithful witness will not lie: but a false witness will utter lies. . . . Go from the presence of a foolish man, when thou perceivest not in him the lips of knowledge. . . . The simple believeth every word: but the prudent man looketh well to his going. . . . In all labor there is profit: but the talk of the lips tendeth only to penury. . . . A true witness delivereth souls: but a deceitful witness speaketh lies" (14:3,5,7,15,23,25).

"A soft answer turneth away wrath: but grievous words stir up anger. The tongue of the wise useth knowledge aright: but the mouth of fools poureth out foolishness. . . . The lips of the wise disperse knowledge: but the heart of the foolish doeth not so. . . . A man hath joy by the answer of his mouth: and a word spoken in due season, how good is it! . . . The thoughts of the wicked are an abomination to the LORD: but the words of the pure are pleasant words. . . . The heart of the righteous studieth to answer: but the mouth of the wicked poureth out evil things. . . . The light of the eyes rejoiceth the heart: and a good report maketh the bones fat" (15:1,2,7,23,26,28,30).

"The preparations of the heart in man, and the answer of the tongue, is from the Lord. . . . A divine sentence is in the lips of the king: his mouth transgresseth not in judgment. . . . Righteous lips are the delight of kings: and they love him that speaketh right. . . . The wise in heart shall be called prudent: and the sweetness of the lips increaseth learning. . . . The heart of the wise teacheth his mouth, and addeth learning to his lips. Pleasant words are as a honeycomb, sweet to the soul, and health to the bones. . . . An ungodly man diggeth up evil: and in his lips there is as a burning fire. A froward man soweth strife: and a whisperer separateth chief friends. . . . He shutteth his eyes to devise froward things: moving his lips he bringeth evil to pass" (16:1,10,13,21,23,24,27,28,30).

"He that covereth a transgression seeketh love; but he that repeateth a matter separateth very friends. . . . He that hath a froward heart findeth no good: and he that hath a perverse tongue falleth into mischief. . . . He that hath knowledge spareth his words: and a man of understanding is of an excellent spirit. Even a fool, when he holdeth his peace, is counted wise: and he that shutteth his lips is esteemed a man of understanding" (17:9,20, 27,28).

"The words of a man's mouth are as deep waters, and the well-spring of wisdom as a flowing brook. . . . A fool's lips enter into contention, and his mouth calleth for strokes. A fool's mouth is his destruction, and his lips are the snare of his soul. The words of a talebearer are as wounds, and they go down into the innermost parts of the belly. . . . He that answereth a matter before he heareth it, it is folly and shame unto him. . . . He that is first in his own cause seemeth just; but his neighbor cometh and searcheth him. . . . A man's belly shall be satisfied with the fruit of his mouth; and with the increase of his lips shall he be filled. Death and life are in the power of the tongue: and they that love it shall eat the fruit thereof. . . . The poor useth entreaties; but the rich answereth roughly" (18:4,6-8,13,17,20-21,23).

"Most men will proclaim every one his own goodness: but a faithful man who can find? . . . It is naught, it is naught, saith the buyer: but when he is gone his way, then he boasteth. . . . Bread of deceit is sweet to a man; but afterwards his mouth shall be filled with gravel. . . . He that goeth about as a talebearer revealeth secrets: therefore meddle not with him that flattereth with his lips. Whoso curseth his father or his mother, his lamp shall be put out in obscure darkness. . . . Say not thou, I will recompense evil; but wait on the Lord, and he shall save thee. . . . It is a snare to the man who devoureth that which is holy, and after vows to make inquiry" (20:6,14,17,19,20, 22,25).

"The getting of treasures by a lying tongue is a vanity tossed to and fro of them that seek death. . . . Whoso keepeth his mouth and his tongue keepeth his soul from troubles. . . . A false witness shall perish: but the man that heareth speaketh constantly" (21:6,23,28).

"He that loveth pureness of heart, for the grace of his lips the king shall be his friend. The eyes of the LORD preserve knowledge, and he overthroweth the words of the transgressor" (22:11-12).

"He that saith unto the wicked, Thou art righteous; him shall the people curse, nations shall abhor him: But to them that rebuke him shall be delight, and a good blessing shall come upon them. Every man shall kiss his lips that giveth a right answer. . . . Be not a witness against thy neighbor without a cause; and deceive not with thy lips" (24:24-26,28).

"Debate thy cause with thy neighbor himself; and discover not a secret to another: Lest he that heareth it put thee to shame, and thine infamy turn not away. A word fitly spoken is like apples of gold in pictures of silver. . . . As the cold of snow in the time of harvest, so is a faithful messenger to them that send him: for he refresheth the soul of his masters. Whoso boasteth himself of a false gift is like clouds and wind without rain. By long forbearing is a prince persuaded, and a soft tongue breaketh the bone. . . . A man that beareth false witness against his neighbor is a maul, and a sword, and a sharp arrow. . . . As he that taketh away a garment in cold weather, and as vinegar upon nitre, so is he that singeth songs to a heavy heart. . . . The north wind driveth away rain: so doth an angry countenance a backbiting tongue. It is better to dwell in the corner of the housetop, than with a brawling woman in a wide house. As cold waters to a thirsty soul, so is good news from a far country" (25:9-11,13-15,18,20,23-25).

"Answer not a fool according to his folly, lest thou also be like unto him. Answer a fool according to his folly, lest he be wise in his own conceit. . . . As a mad man who casteth firebrands, arrows, and death, So is the man that deceiveth his neighbor, and saith, Am I not in sport? Where no wood is, there the fire goeth out: so where there is no talebearer, the strife ceaseth. . . .The words of a talebearer are as wounds, and they go down into the inner most parts of the belly. Burning lips and a wicked heart are like a potsherd covered with silver dross. He that hateth dissembleth with his lips, and layeth up deceit within him; When he speaketh fair, believe him not: for there are seven abominations in his heart. . . . A lying tonue hateth those that are afflicted by it; and a flattering mouth worketh ruin" (26:4,5,18-20,22-25,28).

"Boast not thyself of tomorrow; for thou knowest not what a day may bring forth. Let another man praise thee, and not thine own mouth; a stranger, and not thine own lips. . . . He that blesseth his friend with a loud voice, rising early in the morning, it shall be counted a curse to him. A continual dropping in a very rainy day and a contentious woman are alike" (27:1, 2,14,15).

"He that rebuketh a man afterwards shall find more favor than he that flattereth with the tongue" (28:23).

"A man that flattereth his neighbor spreadeth a net for his feet. . . . A fool uttereth all his mind: but a wise man keepeth it in till afterwards. . . . A servant will not be corrected by words: for though he understand he will not answer. Seest thou a man that is hasty in his words? There is more hope of a fool than of him" (29:5,11,19,20).

"Open thy mouth for the dumb in the cause of all such as are appointed to destruction. Open thy mouth, judge righteously, and plead the cause of the poor and needy. Who can find a virtuous woman? . . . She openeth her mouth with wisdom; and in her tongue is the law of kindness" (31:8-9,10a,26).

CASTING LIGHT ON THESE VERSES

1. What do these words mean: *froward, perverse, prating, contentious?* _____

   _____

   _____

   _____

   _____

2. Underline all the phrases in these verses which speak of a good use of words.
3. With a different colored pencil, underline all the phrases which speak of a bad use of words.
4. With a third colored pencil, underline all references to falsehood.
5. With a fourth colored pencil, underline all references to holding the tongue or keeping silence.
6. Find at least five principles for good Christian conversation as indicated in these verses._____

   _____

   _____

   _____

   _____

   _____

7. Find at least five warnings about unwise speech in these verses. _____

_____

_____

_____

_____

8. What is meant by "the fruit of the mouth" (13:2; 18:20-21)? _____

_____

_____

9. How is a word aptly spoken like apples of gold in a silver bowl or in a picture of silver (25:11)? _____

_____

_____

10. Pretend you are an advice columnist and match at least one of these proverbs with situations that people might write about. What advice would you give after studying these verses? *Example:*

Dear Ann Abigail,

At a party I met a man who talked nonstop and didn't know what he was talking about. I was trapped and bored. What should I have done?"

Answer: You should have excused yourself and gone away (14:7).

_____

_____

MORE LIGHT FROM THE BIBLE

11. Look up the following references and write down what you learn about how the Lord wants us to speak:

    Psalm 35:28 _____

    Psalm 39:1 _____

    Psalm 49:3 _____

    Psalm 119:172 _____

    Psalm 145 _____

    Acts 1:8 _____

    1 Corinthians 13:1 _____

    Ephesians 5:19-20 _____

    Colossians 4:6 _____

    James 1:19 _____

12. What do the following verses warn against?

    Exodus 20:7,16 _____

    Ephesians 5:4,11-12 _____

    Titus 3:2,9 _____

    James 1:26; 4:11 _____

13. Why is proper and righteous speech so important (Matt. 12:35-37; James 2:12-13)? _____

    _____

    _____

14. James 3:1-6 stresses the power of the tongue (see also

Prov. 25:15). Are words more powerful than deeds?___

_____

_____

15. James compares the tongue to a fire (James 3:5-6). Fire can be used in good and bad ways. Compare the uses of fire and the ways words can be used to help or hurt. ___

_____

_____

_____

LIGHT FOR OUR LIVES

16. Do you believe that "silence is golden"? (See Prov. 10:19; 17:27,28.) Do you think it is better to talk things out or to suppress them? _____

_____

_____

17. We are warned against dishonesty and the flattery of fools (Prov. 12:22; 14:25; 19:5; 26:28; 29:5). Should Christians be brutally frank at all times? Consider Proverbs 11:9; 12:18; 28:23; 31:26. _____

_____

_____

_____

_____

18. What are the ingredients of good communication? What are its results?_____

_____

14

MARRIAGE

"When wisdom entereth into thine heart, and knowledge is pleasant unto thy soul; Discretion shall preserve thee, understanding shall keep thee: To deliver thee from the way of the evil man, from the man that speaketh froward things . . . To deliver thee from the strange woman, even from the stranger which flattereth with her words: Which forsaketh the guide of her youth, and forgetteth the covenant of her God" (Proverbs 2:10-12,16-17).

"The curse of the LORD is in the house of the wicked: but he blesseth the habitation of the just" (3:33).

"Let thy fountain be blessed: and rejoice with the wife of thy youth. Let her be as the loving hind and pleasant roe; let her breasts satisfy thee at all times; and be thou ravished always with her love. And why wilt thou, my son, be ravished with a strange woman, and embrace the bosom of a stranger? For the ways of man are before the eyes of the LORD, and he pondereth all his goings" (5:18-21).

"For the commandment is a lamp; and the law is light; and reproofs of instruction are the way of life: To keep thee from the evil woman, from the flattery of the tongue of a strange woman. Lust not after her beauty in thine heart; neither let her take thee with her eyelids. For by means of a whorish woman a man is brought to a piece of bread: and the adulteress will hunt for the precious life. Can a man take fire in his bosom, and his clothes not be burned? Can one go upon hot coals, and his feet not be burned? So he that goeth in to his neighbor's wife; whosoever toucheth her shall not be innocent. Men do not despise a thief, if he steal to satisfy his soul when he is hungry; But if he be found, he shall restore sevenfold; he shall give all the substance of his house. But whoso committeth adultery with a woman lacketh understanding: he that doeth it destroyeth his own soul. A wound and dishonor shall he get; and his reproach shall not be wiped away. For jealousy is the rage of a man: therefore he will not spare in the day of vengeance. He will not regard any ransom; neither will he rest content, though thou givest many gifts" (6:23-35).

"Say unto wisdom, Thou art my sister; and call understanding thy kins-woman: That they may keep thee from the strange woman, from the stranger which flattereth with her words. For at the window of my house I looked through my casement, And beheld among the simple ones, I discerned among the youths, a young man void of understanding, Passing through the street near her corner; and he went the way to her house, In the twilight, in the evening, in the black and dark night: And, behold, there met him a woman with the attire of a harlot, and subtle of heart. (She is loud and stubborn; her feet abide not in her house; Now is she without, now in the streets, and lieth in wait at every corner.) So she caught him, and kissed him, and with an impudent face said unto him, I have peace offerings with me; this day have I paid my vows. Therefore came I forth to meet thee, diligently to seek thy face, and I have found thee. I have decked my bed with coverings of tapestry, with carved works, with fine linen of Egypt. I have perfumed my bed with myrrh, aloes, and cinnamon. Come, let us take our fill of love until the morning: let us solace ourselves with loves. For the goodman is not at home, he is gone a long journey: He hath taken a bag of money with him, and will come home at the day appointed. With her much fair speech she caused him to yield, with the flattering of her lips she forced him. He goeth after her straightway, as an ox goeth to the slaughter, or as a fool to the correction of the stocks; Till a dart strike through his liver; as a bird hasteth to the snare, and knoweth not that it is for his life. Hearken unto me now therefore, O ye children, and attend to the words of my mouth. Let not thine heart decline to her ways, go not astray in her paths. For she hath cast down many wounded: yea, many strong men have been slain by her. Her house is the way to hell, going down to the chambers of death" (7:4-27).

"A virtuous woman is a crown to her husband: but she that maketh ashamed is as rottenness in his bones" (12:4).

"Every wise woman buildeth her house: but the foolish plucketh it down with her hands. . . . The house of the wicked shall be overthrown: but the tabernacle of the upright shall flourish" (14:1,11).

"Whoso findeth a wife findeth a good thing, and obtaineth favor of the LORD" (18:22).

"A foolish son is the calamity of his father: and the contentions of a wife are a continual dropping. House and riches are the inheritance of fathers: and a prudent wife is from the LORD" (19:13,14).

"It is better to dwell in a corner of the housetop, than with a brawling woman in a wide house. . . . It is better to dwell in the wilderness, than with a contentious and an angry woman" (21:9,19).

"Look not thou upon the wine when it is red, when it giveth his color in the cup, when it moveth itself aright. . . . Thine eyes shall behold strange women, and thine heart shall utter perverse things" (23:31,33).

"As coals are to burning coals, and wood to fire; so is a contentious man to kindle strife" (26:21).

"A continual dropping in a very rainy day and a contentious woman are alike. Whosoever hideth her hideth the wind, and the ointment of his right hand, which bewrayeth itself" (27:15-16).

"There be three things which are too wonderful for me, yea, four which I know not: The way of an eagle in the air; the way of a serpent upon a rock; the way of a ship in the midst of the sea; and the way of a man with a maid. Such is the way of an adulterous woman; she eateth, and wipeth her mouth, and saith, I have done no wickedness. For three things the earth is disquieted, and for four which it cannot bear: For a servant when he reigneth; and a fool when he is filled with meat; For an odious woman when she is married; and a handmaid that is heir to her mistress" (30:18-23).

"Who can find a virtuous woman? for her price is far above rubies. The heart of her husband doth safely trust in her, so that he shall have no need of spoil. She will do him good and not evil all the days of her life. She seeketh wool, and flax, and worketh willingly with her hands. She is like the merchants' ships; she bringeth her food from afar. She riseth also while it is yet night, and giveth meat to her household, and a portion to her maidens. She considereth a field, and buyeth it: with the fruit of her hands she planteth a vineyard. She girdeth her loins with strength, and strengtheneth her arms. She perceiveth that her merchandise is good: her candle goeth not out by night. She layeth her hands to the spindle, and her hands hold the distaff. She stretcheth out her hand to the poor; yea, she reacheth forth her hands to the needy. She is not afraid of the snow for her household: for all her household are clothed with scarlet. She maketh herself coverings of tapestry; her clothing is silk and purple. Her husband is known in the gates, when he sitteth among the elders of the land. She maketh fine linen, and selleth it; and delivereth girdles unto the merchant. Strength and honor are her clothing; and she shall rejoice in time to come. She openeth her mouth with wisdom; and in her tongue is the law of kindness. She looketh well to the way of her household, and eateth not the bread of idleness. Her children arise up, and call her blessed; her husband also, and he praiseth her. Many daughters have done virtuously, but thou excellest them all. Favor is deceitful, and beauty is vain: but a woman that feareth the Lord, she shall be praised. Give her of the fruit of her hands; and let her own works praise her in the gates" (31:10-31).

CASTING LIGHT ON THESE VERSES

1. What things are mentioned in these verses that make a happy marriage?_____

_____

_____

2. What things are suggested that break down a marriage?

_____

_____

3. What things are mentioned in the verses from chapter 2 which help one choose a marriage partner? _____

_____

_____

4. The word *knowledge* is used in 2:10. What kind of knowledge is necessary for a good marriage? How can you know and understand your mate better? _____

_____

_____

_____

5. What essentials for a happy home are given in 3:33?

_____

6. According to 5:17-21, how should Christians view the sexual relationship between husband and wife: as a blessing? as a duty? as a result of sin? as a means of communication? as a necessity for the conception of children? as a joy?_____

_____

_____

7. Read 6:23-35. Sexual sins always seem to receive more attention than other sins. Why is this true? _____

_____

Why can nothing material be an adequate payment for this sin (v. 35)?_____

_____

_____

Is jealousy a good or evil force in a marriage (v. 34)?

_____

_____

Can anyone ever truly forgive an unfaithful mate?_____

_____

8. The verses quoted from chapter 7 vividly tell of the betrayal of a marriage. If you read these verses from *The Living Bible,* you will notice immediately that they could almost be a newspaper report of an eyewitness's testimony today. What factors could make a wife promiscuous?_____

_____

_____

What could make a husband fall for her temptation?

_____

_____

Why did she make such a lovely setting for this sin?____

_____

_____

Can anyone ever sin sexually and not suffer for it (v. 23)?

_____

_____

9. Read 27:15-16 in other versions. Now read 26:21. Arguments and fights make marriage unbearable. God loves peace and order. Can a quarrelsome husband or a wife who constantly picks fights be cured? If so, how? _____

_____

_____

10. Why is the "way of a man with a maid" too wonderful to understand (30:19)?_____

_____

_____

11. Notice how the adulterous woman justifies herself in 3:20. How do people justify the "new morality" today?

_____

_____

_____

12. The NIV of 30:23 reads, "an unloved woman who is married. . . ." Why is an unloved wife hard to bear? Notice Leah's grief in Genesis 29:31-35. Notice also the command in Ephesians 5:25,28._____

_____

13. List the attributes of the ideal wife as given in 31:10-31.

_____

_____

_____

_____

_____

a. Must a woman strive to have all of these attributes?

_____

b. Is there no rest for a good wife (31:18)?_____

_____

c. Explore the meaning of this verse. What is her best attribute? _____

_____

d. What kind of husband deserves this kind of wife?

_____

e. How can husbands and wives bring out the best in one another? _____

_____

_____

MORE LIGHT FROM THE BIBLE

14. Abigail was a virtuous woman who had a gruff, vulgar, foolish husband (1 Sam. 25:3). Read the whole chapter and decide if she was right to act behind her husband's back. _____

_____

_____

15. Ahab had a very wicked wife. Did she act out of true love

for her husband (1 Kings 21:1-16)?_____

_____

16. Read Jeremiah 3. How was Israel like an unfaithful wife?

_____

_____

How did God feel about this unfaithfulness?_____

_____

_____

Was He ready to forgive (Jer. 3:12,14)?_____

_____

What was required of the unfaithful people (Jer. 3:13)?

_____

How can this be applied to Christians whose marriages are torn by adultery? _____

_____

_____

17. What does Paul recommend in 1 Corinthians 7:2-5 as a precaution against adultery?_____

_____

18. Can an unbeliever and a believer have a happy marriage? Should they fight about religion? See 2 Corinthians 6:14; 1 Corinthians 7:12-16; 1 Peter 3:1-2. _____

_____

_____

19. Is a gentle, loving husband unmanly? See Ephesians 5:28-33 and 1 Peter 3:7. _____

_____

20. Both 1 Peter 3:1 and verse 7 (RSV) begin with the word *likewise*. To whom does this word refer?_____

_____

21. Should a woman feel degraded or inferior if she is subject or submissive to her husband as the head of their marriage (1 Peter 3:1; Eph. 5:22-24)?_____

_____

_____

22. Is subjection only for wives (Eph. 5:21)? _____

_____

23. Name every way that you can in which a Christian marriage can resemble the relationship of Christ and the church. See Ephesians 5:21-33. _____

_____

_____

LIGHT FOR OUR LIVES

24. Does spiritual growth and compatibility enhance or detract from the marriage relationship? Or do you feel closer to your mate when you feel closer to the Lord? _____

_____

_____

_____

25. Privately review your own marriage and evaluate it in the light of what has been learned in this lesson. What can you do to make your marriage more Christlike and happier so it will be a witness to others of God's love? _____

_____

_____

_____

_____

15

WALKING IN THE WAY

"My son, if sinners entice thee, consent thou not. . . . My son, walk not thou in the way with them; refrain thy foot from their path: For their feet run to evil, and make haste to shed blood" (Proverbs 1:10,15-16).

"My son, if thou wilt receive my words, and hide my commandments with thee; . . . Then shalt thou understand righteousness, and judgment, and equity; yea, every good path. . . . Discretion shall preserve thee, understanding shall keep thee: To deliver thee from the way of the evil man, from the man that speaketh froward things; Who leave the paths of uprightness, to walk in the ways of darkness; Who rejoice to do evil, and delight in the frowardness of the wicked; Whose ways are crooked, and they froward in their paths: . . . That thou mayest walk in the way of good men, and keep the paths of the righteous" (2:1,9,11-15,20).

"Trust in the LORD with all thine heart; and lean not unto thine own understanding. In all thy ways acknowledge him, and he shall direct thy paths. . . . Happy is the man that findeth wisdom, and the man that getteth understanding . . . Her ways are ways of pleasantness, and all her paths are peace. . . . My son, let not them depart from thine eyes: keep sound wisdom and discretion: So shall they be life unto thy soul, and grace to thy neck. Then shalt thou walk in thy way safely, and thy foot shall not stumble. . . . For the LORD shall be thy confidence, and shall keep thy foot from being taken" (3:5-6,13,17,21-23,26).

"I have taught thee in the way of wisdom; I have led thee in right paths. When thou goest, thy steps shall not be straitened; and when thou runnest, thou shalt not stumble. . . . Enter not into the path of the wicked, and go not in the way of evil men. Avoid it, pass not by it, turn from it, and pass away. . . . But the path of the just is as the shining light, that shineth more and more unto the perfect day. The way of the wicked is as darkness: they know not at what they stumble. . . . Ponder the path of thy feet, and let all thy ways be established. Turn not to the right hand nor to the left: remove thy foot from evil" (4:11-12,14-15,18-19,26-27).

"For the lips of a strange woman drop as a honeycomb, and her mouth is smoother than oil: . . . Her feet go down to death; her steps take hold on hell. Lest thou shouldest ponder the path of life, her ways are moveable, that thou canst not know them. Hear me now therefore, O ye children, and depart not from the words of my mouth. Remove thy way far from her, and come not nigh the door of her house: . . . For the ways of man are before the eyes of the LORD, and he pondereth all his goings" (5:3,5-8,21).

"For the commandment is a lamp; and the law is light; and reproofs of instruction are the way of life" (6:23).

"Doth not wisdom cry? and understanding put forth her voice? She standeth in the top of high places, by the way in the places of the paths. . . . I lead in the way of righteousness, in the midst of the paths of judgment: . . . Now therefore hearken unto me, O ye children: for blessed are they that keep my ways" (8:1-2,20,32).

"Forsake the foolish, and live; and go in the way of understanding" (9:6).

"He that walketh uprightly walketh surely: but he that perverteth his ways shall be known. . . . He is in the way of life that keepeth instruction: but he that refuseth reproof erreth. . . . The way of the LORD is strength to the upright: but destruction shall be to the workers of iniquity" (10:9,17,29).

"The righteousness of the perfect shall direct his way: but the wicked shall fall by his own wickedness. . . . They that are of a froward heart are abomination to the LORD: but such as are upright in their way are his delight" (11:5,20).

"The way of a fool is right in his own eyes: but he that hearkeneth unto counsel is wise. . . . The righteous is more excellent than his neighbor: but the way of the wicked seduceth them. . . . In the way of righteousness is life; and in the pathway thereof there is no death" (12:15,26,28).

"Righteousness keepeth him that is upright in the way: but wickedness overthroweth the sinner. . . . Good understanding giveth favor: but the way of transgressors is hard. . . . He that walketh with wise men shall be wise: but a companion of fools shall be destroyed" (13:6,15,20).

"He that walketh in his uprightness feareth the LORD: but he that is perverse in his ways despiseth him. . . . The wisdom of the prudent is to understand his way: but the folly of fools is deceit. . . . There is a way which seemeth right unto a man, but the end thereof are the ways of death" (14:2,8,12).

"The way of the wicked is an abomination unto the LORD: but he loveth him that followeth after righteousness. Correction is grievous unto him that forsaketh the way: and he that hateth reproof shall die. . . . The way of the slothful man is as a hedge of thorns: but the way of the righteous is made plain. . . . The way of life is above to the wise, that he may depart from hell beneath" (15:9,10,19,24).

"A man's heart deviseth his way: but the LORD directeth his steps. . . . The highway of the upright is to depart from evil: he that keepeth his way preserveth his soul. . . . There is a way that seemeth right unto a man, but the end thereof are the ways of death. . . . A violent man enticeth his neighbor, and leadeth him into the way that is not good. . . . The hoary head is a crown of glory, if it be found in the way of righteousness" (16:9,17,25,29,31).

"The just man walketh in his integrity: his children are blessed after him. . . . Man's goings are of the Lord; how can a man then understand his own way?" (20:7,24).

"Every way of a man is right in his own eyes: but the Lord pondereth the hearts. . . . The way of man is froward and strange: but as for the pure, his work is right. . . . The man that wandereth out of the way of understanding shall remain in the congregation of the dead. . . . A wicked man hardeneth his face: but as for the upright, he directeth his way" (21:2,8,16,29).

"Train up a child in the way he should go: and when he is old, he will not depart from it" (22:6).

"Hear thou, my son, and be wise, and guide thine heart in the way" (23:19).

"Whoso causeth the righteous to go astray in an evil way, he shall fall himself into his own pit: but the upright shall have good things in possession. . . . Whoso walketh uprightly shall be saved: but he that is perverse in his ways shall fall at once. . . . He that trusteth in his own heart is a fool: but whoso walketh wisely, he shall be delivered" (28:10,18,26).

"An unjust man is an abomination to the just: and he that is upright in the way is abomination to the wicked" (29:27).

CASTING LIGHT ON THESE VERSES

1. Find at least two verses in this lesson which cite God as our guide in life. _____

   _____

   _____

2. Find three or more verses which warn against the influence of evil companions in our travels through life.

   _____

3. Which verse in chapter 2 tells what our "roadmap" should be?_____

   _____

   _____

4. The scorner is described in 2:11-15. How are we to deal with scorners? See Matthew 18:15-17. _____

_____

_____

5. Do these verses (1:15; 4:14-15,27) advocate complete separation from unbelievers? _____

_____

6. Contrast the way of light with the way of darkness in 4:18-19; 13:15; 15:19; 28:18. _____

_____

_____

7. Where does each of these ways end? See 5:5; 12:28; 15:24; 21:16. _____

_____

_____

8. According to the verses in our lesson, what benefits are enjoyed by those who walk in God's way?_____

_____

_____

_____

9. Read 5:6 in other translations, because the KJV of this verse is difficult. _____

_____

_____

10. What warning and comfort do you find in these verses: 5:21; 12:15; 14:12; 16:2,17; 21:2? _____

_____

_____

MORE LIGHT FROM THE BIBLE

11. Which verse in Psalm 119 is similar to Proverbs 6:23?

_____

12. In Matthew 7:13-14, Jesus contrasts the broad and the narrow ways. Imagine that you can travel to a certain city by expressway or by an old two-lane highway. How would these roads differ? Now try to draw spiritual parallels or comparisons to our travels through life. _____

_____

_____

_____

_____

_____

13. In John 14:6 we read Jesus' words, "I am the way, the truth, and the life: no man cometh unto the Father but by me." How is Jesus the way or path to God? _____

_____

_____

LIGHT FOR OUR LIVES

14. Proverbs 7:25 (NIV) reads, "Do not let your heart turn to her ways or stray into her paths." Read the following

verses in order: Mark 7:20-23; Matthew 5:22,28; Philippians 4:8; Proverbs 12:5; 23:19. What forces in the world today pressure us to choose the wrong way? How can we protect ourselves and our children from these bad influences? _____

_____

_____

_____

_____

15. There are hundreds of verses in the Bible which speak of the "way." Using a Bible concordance, look up some of the verses listed under "way," or "walk, walked, walketh" and find five that speak to you that you can share with the group._____

_____

_____

_____

_____

_____